What people are saying about

Thoughts of God

A terrific Lent Course inviting us to explore the Biblical theme of being at home and in exile, how beauty and science connect with faith in God, and the astounding relationship a young Hindu had with mathematics. Using Matt Brown's 2015 film *The Man Who Knew Infinity*, as both a launch point but also with its own profound observation of academic life in Cambridge in 1914, Andy Colebrooke takes us on a unique journey of our own Christian faith through the life of Srinivasa Ramanujan, who said, 'An equation means nothing to me unless it expresses a thought of God.'
Stephen Cottrell, Archbishop of York.

A highly original and extremely practical resource for the Church, especially for film lovers. It will take you deep it into the Christian faith. Buy it and use it!
Jeremy Begbie, Director, Duke Initiatives in Theology and the Arts, Duke Divinity School, Durham, North Carolina, U.S.A.

Lent is an opportunity to engage with questions of God and what it means to be human at a deeper level. This book provides an imaginative and stimulating way in, both for individual and group study. For some it will be surprising, for some it will be challenging, but the stories represented in movies can lead us deeper into discovering who we are in the light of a God who loves and redeems. I commend this book to you.
Revd Professor David Wilkinson, Principal of St John's College and Professor of Theology and Religion, Durham University.

Thoughts of God is a first-rate group Lenten study putting Scripture into meaningful and delightful conversation with the film,

The Man Who Knew Infinity (2015). Theology is at its core the conversation between God's story and our stories. That is, as we experience, what the best of sermons do each week. To deepen that conversation, Colebrooke has brought together relevant scriptural texts with the real-life story of the Hindu mathematician Ramanujan's interaction with the Cambridge don and atheist G. H. Hardy. As the film invites viewers to empathize with the humanity of this young Indian family, it encourages us to extend our theological probings concerning our own humanity. Here is the dialogue between Bible and film at its best. Highly recommended.

Robert K. Johnston, Senior Professor of Theology and Culture, Fuller Theological Seminary, and author of *Reel Spirituality* (2006), *God's Wider Presence* (2014), and *God in the Movies* (2017), with Catherine Barsotti).

This Lent course is refreshingly original and yet highly relevant and contemporary to many of the issues facing society and the Christian church today. I knew nothing of Srinivasa Ramanujan until I was sent this book, but his life and work, wonderfully portrayed in the film, has been beautifully woven into the five sessions that make for a truly engaging course. The complexity of the mathematics doesn't interfere with understanding an exciting and intriguing story, that will encourage some lively and fruitful conversations, and I will be recommending it to parishes in my patch.

The Venerable Robin King, Archdeacon of Stansted.

If you are looking for a Lent Course which explores discipleship and the interface between religious faith and the scientific endeavour in a fresh and creative way, *Thoughts of God* is for you. Anchored in a friendship which featured in a 2015 movie, *The Man Who Knew Infinity*, this new course illuminates philosophical and theological truths and tensions in a way which speaks to both head and heart and is anchored in everyday human realities.

The Rt Revd Dr Lee Rayfield, Society of Ordained Scientists, Bishop of Swindon.

Ian Stewart, Emeritus Professor of Mathematics at Warwick University and a Fellow of the Royal Society, said that 'Mathematics is the Cinderella science: undervalued, underestimated, and misunderstood. Yet it has been one of the main driving forces behind human society for at least three millennia, it powers all of today's technology, and it underpins almost every aspect of our daily lives.' (The Guardian, 18 January, 2012). Srinivasa Ramanujan was a self-taught genius from India with a flair for extraordinary and beautiful formulas. A 'Cinderella science' combined with an account of the brief life of a young and impoverished Hindu might seem an odd choice for the subject of a blockbuster movie, let alone for a Lent Course. However, the movie is compelling – and it deals with everything from the nature of truth, the life of faith and the evils of racism to the importance of relationships and the inescapable matter of our own mortality. And this course draws upon those issues, as well as the themes of exile and homecoming, and delivers a thought-provoking and rich exploration into what it means to live, love, and believe in the twenty-first century.

As we emerge from the trauma, losses, and deprivations of the COVID pandemic, many of us are asking deep and searching questions about the very issues raised in this course. And just like the discipline of mathematics, this course is not just about finding answers; it is also about understanding why answers exist in the first place, and why they might take the form they do. Like mathematicians, we are not just concerned with understanding the world; we are also looking to open up new worlds of possibility – and maybe to find hope amidst the devastation and disillusionment of our post-pandemic world. This exciting, challenging, and inspirational course will help us to do just that. In five easy-to-follow sessions, the elegantly written material provides everything participants will need in order to engage with the fundamental issues of life, love and faith. It all adds up to an excellent course.

The Rt Revd Roger Morris, Area Bishop of Colchester.

By the same author

Science and Religion: The Spirituality of James Clerk Maxwell,
Grove Books, Cambridge 2020
ISBN 978-1-78827-112-7

Thoughts of God

Exile, truth, and the longing for home
A Lent Course based on the film
The Man Who Knew Infinity

Thoughts of God

Exile, truth, and the longing for home
A Lent Course based on the film
The Man Who Knew Infinity

Andy Colebrooke

CIRCLE
BOOKS

Winchester, UK
Washington, USA

JOHN HUNT PUBLISHING

First published by Circle Books, 2022
Circle Books is an imprint of John Hunt Publishing Ltd., No. 3 East St., Alresford,
Hampshire SO24 9EE, UK
office@jhpbooks.com
www.johnhuntpublishing.com
www.circle-books.com

For distributor details and how to order please visit the 'Ordering' section on our website.

Text copyright: Andy Colebrooke 2021

ISBN: 978 1 78535 971 2
978 1 78535 972 9 (ebook)
Library of Congress Control Number: 2021944416

A CIP catalogue record for this book is available from the British Library.

Design: Stuart Davies

UK: Printed and bound by CPI Group (UK) Ltd, Croydon, CR0 4YY
US: Printed and bound by Thomson Shore, 7300 West Joy Road, Dexter, MI 48130

We operate a distinctive and ethical publishing philosophy in
all areas of our business, from our global network of authors to
production and worldwide distribution.

Contents

An equation means nothing to me unless it expresses a thought of God.
Srinivasa Ramanujan

Introduction

'Thoughts of God'? By that I mean both thoughts about God, and perhaps more presumptuously, God's own thoughts. Thoughts about God come under the heading of theology: what we can legitimately say about God and God's relation to the world, summarised in a series of doctrines. God's own thoughts cannot be known unless God chooses to reveal them. Those thoughts are the ones God articulates for us through his word, through nature, through personal revelation, and supremely through his Son, Jesus Christ. Both meanings of the title will find their place in this five-week Lent course as it looks at the intriguing story of two very different personalities, who worked together at the time of the first world war: Srinivasa Ramanujan, a mathematics phenomenon from Madras in India, and the Cambridge don G. H. Hardy. One believed that thoughts about God were irrational, the other believed that God's thoughts came to him as he worshipped or slept. The gulf between these two men was initially vast, but through their shared passion for numbers they were drawn together into the thrill of discovery. Matt Brown's film, *The Man Who Knew Infinity* (2015), captures the excitement of those far off days, presenting us with an absorbing tale of their time together. However, it may strike some as strange that a Lent course has been based on the lives of an atheist and a Hindu! The reason behind my choice is that their story is easily relatable to five major Bible themes: journeying in faith; exile and return; questions about truth; friendship with God; and the longing for an eternal home. The film thus provides natural stepping off points for groups to explore these themes and apply them to their own Christian lives; opportunities to explore incarnation, cross and resurrection follow naturally.

The power of a story to communicate with an audience first really struck me when I visited Marrakech in the early 1970s.

It seemed like stepping back into Bible times; in the evenings in the market square storytellers entertained crowds, who sat cross-legged on the ground, totally absorbed by the storyteller's art. It was a most potent demonstration to me of the importance of stories, myths, and fairy tales, in captivating audiences and leaving a lasting impression. All preachers know, or should know, the power of a good story to engage a congregation: as soon as the sermon turns didactic and is filled with bullet points, there is a danger that eyes will glaze over, and nothing memorable will remain. We have, from the very beginning, been creatures who love to hear and tell stories; our brains seem to be hardwired for this way of communicating. When human stories are told, whether heroic or tragic, we cannot help but become engaged. Of course, the Bible writers knew this. Much of God's word comes to us in the form of story; the Bible is filled with the lives of the good, the bad, and the ugly, each one a human being with something to teach us. We also see a nation encountering God, struggling to learn and live by his ways, and, more often than not, failing. This story, too, is recorded for our learning. Finally, in the providence of God, the whole Christian Bible is a meta-narrative of God's salvation plan, centred on the figure of Jesus Christ, climaxing in a glorious future hope with him.

Western literature from Homer to the Victorian novel to Margaret Atwood and Ian McEwan continues to feed an insatiable appetite for drama and an understanding of the human condition. We live now in a very visual age. Cinema and television have become the media through which most people encounter the power of story to reflect human experience. Everyone has got a mobile phone, a tablet, and any number of other devices, so perhaps those Moroccan storytellers have all gone, but the passion for stories of adventure, romance and triumph remains, via TV Soaps, Box Set dramas, NetFlix and Hollywood Blockbusters. Video projectors are now common place in many churches, or can be easily borrowed, making courses based on films a viable option in most contexts. If the Church is to proclaim the gospel afresh to each generation, then it must engage with contemporary visual culture. 'Filmmakers are the storytellers and mythmakers of our culture, and films reflect the contemporary quest for meaning and truth' (Coffey, 1999). Indeed, cinema can be a mirror in which to see ourselves; an invitation to reflect on our own attitudes and shortcomings, prompting the biggest questions, such as *which values are important in life, what makes a good person,* and *where can we find lasting hope?*

Lent, too, is a time for reflection; the season for slowing down, stepping back to take our own spiritual temperature, so as to be better prepared for the celebration of Easter. Through prayer, devotional reading, and self-denial, we try to focus our eyes more sharply on Jesus, resetting our spiritual compass to set out again on the path of following him. Although not true of all Churches, Lent may be the only time when many congregations find an appetite for joining a study group or short course. Finding the right course for a church can be an annual headache for a busy pastor or vicar. What is often looked for is a course that offers a fresh and lively approach, which can sustain enthusiasm and will attract those that other courses just do not reach. This is where cinema can be remarkably effective, for films are invitations to enter human stories and fire the imagination. When we can empathise emotionally with the characters, and see situations through their eyes, then our thoughts turn to the pains, joys, and puzzles of being human. Add to that an encounter with scripture and spiritual growth can occur, particularly if done in conversation with others.

The Covid-19 pandemic has made us all feel a little like exiles longing for a return to normality, but it has also sparked a revolution in the way we do church. To keep going during lockdowns churches have learned to go online, conducting worship via YouTube or Zoom-type video conferencing. Local expertise in the use of such software is now widespread, meaning that homegroups and seasonal courses can be conducted across the internet. This course was written during a lockdown when all church buildings were closed in England; it was then presented using Zoom with the film clips shared from the host's computer. The advantages of this method are the ease of screening and the potential there is to attract participants from a wider geographical area. Of course, when possible, real life interaction is much to be preferred, and this course will work well in either situation.

Part 1 offers a brief outline of the lives of Ramanujan and Hardy, avoiding the impenetrable mathematics that so excited them. Their stories are not widely known and if the film sparks an interest in their real lives, then this summary gives a useful introduction. Part 2 details the nuts and bolts of running the course, whether in a church hall, a living room or shared online. Although it was designed for Lent, it is in fact suitable for any time of year, in a variety of settings. Part 3 contains the course's core material in a regularly structured format. Within it are the film timings, background information, group discussion starters, and questions for personal reflection. Each week has a simple closing liturgy related to the theme. This structure gives the busy leader all that is necessary to run each session, allowing a degree of selectivity about the discussion questions and not preventing the addition of other ideas, if wished. The questions provided may sometimes seem provocative, this is in the hope that they may widen discussion or open doors to fresh insights. My aim has been to keep the text succinct and straightforward: this leaves space for personal note taking, so that readers can record thoughts, questions, or actions. For those interested in going deeper or following up issues hinted at in the course, a postscript is provided, which can be used for an additional meeting or as an opening session for a new homegroup.

My thanks go to those who took part in the two trials of this course: the members of the homegroup that meets at Sue and Graeme's house, and the students from *The Course in Christian Studies* in Chelmsford Diocese, co-led by my colleague The Revd. Angela Want. Most of all I wish to thank Hazel, my wife, for her constant inspiration and encouragement in the writing of this course.

1

Srinivasa Ramanujan and G. H. Hardy

The Man Who Knew Infinity charts the stormy working relationship between an Indian of very humble origins, Srinivasa Ramanujan, and the vastly different Cambridge academic G. H. Hardy. The don shared neither the Indian's love of intuition nor his belief in God, rather his life's focus was on attaining rigorous mathematical proof for all his work. The story ends in both stunning success and tragic loss. The film is based on historical events, but as with all films the makers have necessarily been selective in what they portray, and have adjusted characters and incidents to make a compelling story. Whilst our concern will be with the issues the film raises, here is a very brief, mathematics-free, outline of what we know of the historical Ramanujan and his mentor Hardy.

Ramanujan was born on 22 December, 1887, in Kumbakonam, in the Southern Indian State of Tamil Nadu. His name means 'younger brother of Rama'. His father was a shopkeeper and his mother sang at a local temple; she brought her son up to be an orthodox Brahmin (high caste, but not well off) and therefore a strict vegetarian. From an early age mathematics was Ramanujan's passion and he excelled at it in school; aged 10 he came top in his District's examination paper and was awarded a college scholarship. However, he seriously neglected his other subjects in favour of his own explorations into mathematics, resulting in repeated failure at important college exams, ending his hopes of entering the University at Madras.

At school Ramanujan was lent a very dry textbook by a tutor for the extremely competitive Mathematical Tripos examinations at Cambridge University. It was what you might call a 'crammer', consisting simply of theorem after theorem

(6165 of them), each stated without proof. However, this book fired the young man's mathematical genius, allowing him to absorb a lot of undergraduate mathematics, but without teaching him the importance of proof. Untrammelled by the straitjacket of Western thinking, Ramanujan's mind, with his extraordinary eye for patterns, roamed free across the whole landscape of numbers, as he filled his notebooks with his own mathematical ideas.

A colleague of Hardy, John Littlewood, recalled that in his early days in Cambridge Ramanujan didn't seem to possess a clear-cut idea of what is meant by proof, and 'if the total mixture of evidence and intuition gave him certainty, he looked no further' (Kanigel, 2016: 224). In fact, Ramanujan believed his mathematical insights came to him through revelation, from the Hindu goddess Namagiri, as he slept or prayed. However, views on the importance of religion to Ramanujan do vary: Hardy contended that it was a matter of observance only and not intellectual conviction; others, notably Indian contemporaries, firmly disagreed. It does seem that the sentiment recorded in the film: 'An equation has no meaning for me unless it expresses a thought of God', is well attested as coming from Ramanujan.

Ramanujan's notebooks were instrumental in getting him a low paid job at the Port Authority in Madras. As he had also been successful in getting some work published in the *Journal of the Indian Mathematical Society,* local mathematicians were taking an interest and he was encouraged to write to prominent scholars in England presenting some of his results. G.H. Hardy at Trinity College, Cambridge, received such a letter, and his first impression was that it came from a crackpot or a fraudster, 'although it turned out to be the most remarkable that I have ever received' (Hardy, 1920: 494).

The letter was sent on 16 January, 1913, and Ramanujan introduced himself as a clerk in the Accounts Department of the Port Trust Office at Madras, aged now 'about 23'. Such a vague assessment of his own age was perhaps not a promising start for a letter of introduction to a mathematics don! Hardy might have been tempted to put the letter aside when it went on to explain that, although Ramanujan had not studied mathematics at a university, he had at least completed a school level course in the subject. Thankfully Hardy did not stop reading, but instead went on to discover that on leaving school Ramanujan had devoted much of his spare time to making his own mathematical investigations. These had taken him in new and exciting directions; the work he presented had startled local Indian mathematicians, with some of his results leaving them totally bemused. Ramanujan then respectfully asked Hardy if he would go through the remainder of the letter and, if he thought any of it to be of value, to see that it was published.

What followed was indeed startling. The body of the letter contained about a hundred theorems, page after page of mathematical formulae, some known to Hardy, some clearly wrong, others strangely new and scarcely possible to believe. Hardy shared the letter with his colleague, John Littlewood, who was similarly excited, but also frustrated that no proofs were provided. They were particularly astonished at Ramanujan's claim to have a formula which accurately counted the total number of primes within a given range all the way up to 100 million – something thought to be totally impossible – and to the pair's great annoyance, the formula was not included in the letter! (Ramanujan was to be proved wrong on this count and no such formula has ever been found.) For mathematicians, any conjecture requires rigorous proof in order to be accepted as true. Proof is the necessary language for the communication of all advances in the subject, providing the explanation of how a result has been achieved.

Hardy wrote back to Ramanujan requesting proofs, but none were provided. However, the final equations in the original letter were so thrilling, Hardy invited his Indian correspondent to join him in Cambridge so that the proofs could be worked on and, if successful, published. Hardy knew he had got a man of extraordinary, if idiosyncratic talent, but also one who lacked basic knowledge of much university level mathematics. Again, Hardy would later write of Ramanujan that he was at best 'a half-educated Indian', who had not even attained a 'Failed B.A.' degree. When he arrived in Cambridge he was ignorant of modern European mathematics and he died when his education had hardly begun.

It seemed plain to Hardy that Ramanujan should be invited to join him in Cambridge and the necessary funding was forthcoming from Trinity College and Madras University. After an initial reluctance to travel Ramanujan joined Hardy in April, 1914.

Godfrey Harold Hardy was born on 7 February, 1877, in Cranleigh, in Surrey, and was therefore only in his mid-thirties at the time the film is set – a much younger man than the film portrays. Neither of his parents had been to university but both had a love for mathematics. The boy's mathematical ability was recognised at a young age. When he was just two years old, he is said to have written down the integers from 1 into the millions, and when taken to church passed the time by factorizing the numbers of the hymns. His talent was recognised by the award of a scholarship to attend Winchester College before entering Trinity College, Cambridge, in 1896. There he was prepared for the Mathematical Tripos Examinations, and graduated as fourth highest in his year.

He joined The Cambridge Apostles, an elite debating society whose other members have included such intellectuals as Bertrand Russell, John Maynard Keynes, and Ludwig Wittgenstein. In 1900 Hardy was made a fellow of Trinity, and in 1906 he was appointed to a lectureship that required only six hours teaching a week, leaving ample time for his own mathematical research. This is the stage of his life depicted in the film. At this point Hardy had been working with Littlewood for about three years. It was a collaboration that would last many years and became one of the most successful partnerships in the story of mathematics. It was said at the time that there were only three really great English mathematicians: Hardy, Littlewood, and Hardy-Littlewood.

The film *The Man Who Knew Infinity* paints a dramatic picture of Hardy's mentoring of Ramanujan. Their common passion for a subject and its power to draw together two utterly different men is captured. Here is Hardy, the dry Cambridge intellectual, convinced of his atheism, obsessed with mathematical rigour, but cut off from his emotions. And here is the antithesis: an impulsive, largely uneducated, intuitive Indian, whose insights come to him in dreams, written on his tongue by a Hindu goddess. As the film shows us, neither man had seen anyone quite like the other before, yet they overcame their differences, forged a genuine friendship together, and are able to share in the thrill of new discoveries.

The film is an extraordinary, mysterious, and exciting cinematic adventure, but how closely does it accord with history? The racism in England at the time is graphically portrayed, most strongly through the fictional lecturer Mr Howard. There must be some truth in this: an almost illiterate young man from India would not have been easily received into Cambridge society in 1914, and the unfolding evidence of his extreme brilliance must have been hard for elitist academics to take. However, the real Trinity College feels that much is grossly exaggerated in the film. In particular, the college claims that the portrayal of Major MacMahon is unfair: rather than looking down on Ramanujan he was in fact a great supporter of him from the start. Also, Trinity College says that any 'boxing match' between Hardy and Ramanujan is a fiction, as is Ramanujan's complaint that he had not come to Cambridge to learn mathematics, but to publish his results. In fact, the college says he was very keen to get a Cambridge degree, and Hardy arranged for him to get his B.A. by research, so that he didn't have to attend lectures (Bollobás, 2020: 134).

The film correctly records Ramanujan's struggle to feed himself, the diagnosis of a terminal illness followed by his suicide attempt, and of course, his triumphant successes. Hardy's support in getting his friend's achievements properly recognised is also correct: Ramanujan became a Fellow of the Royal Society in London on 2 May, 1918, and a few months later a Fellow of Trinity College. As soon as the war ended Ramanujan returned to India to be reunited with Janaki, but sadly his condition worsened and he died on 26 April, 1920, aged 32. Years later, Hardy would say of his friend that it was impossible to judge just how great a mathematician he had been, or might have been, had he lived.

Soon after the war Hardy left Cambridge for New College, Oxford, and the Savilian Chair of Geometry at the university. He had become disillusioned with Cambridge, especially with the pro-War attitudes of his colleagues and their behaviour towards Bertrand Russell, the pacifist who had been jailed for his anti-War activities. Oxford was probably the happiest and most creative period of his life, writing more than 100 papers there, including many with Littlewood who had remained in Cambridge. In 1931 when Hardy was 54, he chose to resign his Oxford Chair and return to Cambridge to become Sadleirian Professor of Pure Mathematics and once again a Fellow of Trinity College. There seem to be two reasons for the move. Firstly, the Cambridge professorship was considered more prestigious than the Oxford one. And secondly, if he had stayed at New College, he would have had to give up his rooms upon retirement, whereas returning to Trinity College meant he could live out the rest of his life there. This he did, as indeed did Littlewood.

Godfrey Harold Hardy died on 1 December, 1947. At the

entrance to the College Chapel a brass plaque now commemorates Hardy's life, recording the distinguished contributions he made to teaching at both Oxford and Cambridge, and his undisputed place among the world's best mathematicians (Trinity College Chapel, 2021). Although Hardy is remembered as an outstanding mathematician in his field, towards the end of his life, he would say that his greatest contribution to mathematics was his discovery of Ramanujan. He paid tribute to their fruitful partnership, citing the inspiration Ramanujan had been for his own mathematical research. The Indian's early death had struck him a very severe blow and this is powerfully brought out in the film.

The years Ramanujan spent in England were to be the most fruitful of the Indian's life. He recorded his results in a series of notebooks and only ever published a small portion of his work. After Ramanujan's death, Hardy made a study of these notebooks and published many more results, with the necessary proofs, a work that has since been continued by others. Hardy also lectured widely about Ramanujan's results and helped others form an accurate picture of one of the most outstanding mathematicians of recent times.

In 1976 more than one hundred pages of loose and unordered material, in Ramanujan's handwriting, were found in a box in the Wren Library at Trinity College. These are now known as Ramanujan's 'lost notebook' containing over six hundred mathematical formulae, without proofs. These have given mathematicians much to work on and many of the formulae have now been published together with proofs of their correctness. It has been said the the discovery of this lost notebook has caused as much stir in the mathematical world as would, in a musical context, the discovery of a tenth symphony by Beethoven.

2

How to Run the Course

The Film and the Course

Thoughts of God is a five-week course that is designed to reflect on the Warner Brothers' film: *The Man Who Knew Infinity* (2015), during Lent or at any other time. The film stars Dev Patel and Jeremy Irons in the lead roles, with Toby Jones as Hardy's Cambridge colleague, John Littlewood, and Devika Bhisé as Janaki, Ramanujan's young wife, left behind in India. This is a well-acted, absorbing piece of cinema, which can be enjoyed whether mathematics fascinates or repels you! Many issues relating to Christian spirituality and discipleship arise naturally from viewing it: questions of faith, doubt, proof and certainty; the problems of living in a culture which is indifferent or hostile to your beliefs; the challenges in developing friendships – with others and with God; the substance of the Christian hope.

It is widely held that Ramanujan said: 'An equation means nothing to me unless it expresses a thought of God', and this is brought out in the film. That Ramanujan was convinced that his ground-breaking ideas were not simply his own, but given to him by the Hindu goddess Namagiri, a belief that Hardy could not accept, gives course participants the opportunity to discuss the nature of revelation and the significance of proof. A postscript to the course provides additional material for a follow-up meeting to encourage exploration of the gap between truth and proof, the limitations of mathematics and science, and whether there is any possibility of a fruitful dialogue between Hinduism and Christianity.

The material is suitable for use in any Church or Christian ecumenical gathering. The three basic marks of the faith – incarnation, cross, and resurrection – are woven into the course, making it suitable for use at any time of year, not just during Lent. It will appeal to anyone who enjoys films and wants to explore how the issues raised bear on Christian faith and discipleship. No great knowledge of, or indeed interest in, mathematics is required. There is ample material for five two-hour sessions, and it has been specially written to suit online meeting platforms such as Zoom, as well as face to face meetings.

Over the five weeks of the course, five major Bible themes are explored: journeying in faith; exile and return; questions about truth; friendship with God; and the longing for an eternal home. These themes are highlighted at various points of the film, and some overlap and are revisited in subsequent weeks.

What is needed – a Check List
Now down to practicalities...

1.   Every participant should be strongly encouraged to see the whole film before the course begins. It is currently available on DVD or by live streaming from Amazon, for rent or purchase.

2.   A DVD copy of the film will need to be obtained for screening the clips or for sharing via the internet – providers like Amazon block screen sharing on the Zoom platform.

3.   Course leaders should view the film several times to become thoroughly familiar with the story and the characters. Do not just view the selected clips.

4.   If you wish to show the film to the group before the course begins, make sure it is a private viewing and not one open to the public. This would contravene the maker's copyright licence which allows only private home use. If you wish to show the whole film, say in a church hall, then it should be open to course members only and no others, and it should not involve the purchase of tickets. Showing full-length films for entertainment, outreach

and social events will require appropriate licensing (in the UK that means a PRS for Music licence and a Church Video Licence).

5. If screening in a hall or homegroup, you will need the following equipment. A large television (42 inches is ideal) or projector and screen; the means to play the DVD, either a player integrated into the TV, or a laptop or other computer device, together with a compatible projector (many church rooms and community halls now have projectors built in).

6. Make sure that you have familiarised yourself with the chosen devices and have rehearsed their use carefully so that you can find the selected clips quickly and smoothly.

7. If you decide to use Zoom your church will need their basic licence – the free version cuts off after about 40 minutes.

8. Make sure you know how to screen share and operate breakout rooms. Again, practice makes perfect.

9. Decide on the venue: a home, a hall, or online; agree dates and times of the meetings, avoiding clashes with other church events if possible.

10. Advertise the course, organise signing up arrangements, give a clear cut off date. You need to work out your maximum course size (probably no more than a dozen for a Zoom meeting).

11. Decide how to cover your costs – by charging or seeking donations, or by getting the church to pay.

12. Purchase the required number of books.

On the Day

Participants should be asked to do the Preparatory Reading for each week prior to the meeting. This needs to be communicated to the group before the course begins. The Preparatory Reading acts as a kind of overture, introducing upcoming themes.

There is more material provided than you are likely to need for a two-hour session, particularly if you choose to meet in person. Conversation flows more naturally face to face and may last longer than planned. Zoom classes can be very chatty too, particularly if people know each other well beforehand. The physical setting up of groups, moving chairs, getting settled, and then reconvening afterwards, all take a surprising amount of time. Whilst Zoomers can grab a drink and be back in ten minutes, coffee and chat takes up much more time in a comfortable living room or warm church hall. Therefore, you may need to be selective about the questions you focus on. Do ensure that both clips are seen so that the sense of the story is preserved and try to set the refreshment break so that you have equal contact time before and after it.

The pattern each week is always the same:

Opening worship
Brief recap of last session
Introduction to the theme
First Clip
Whole group and small group work
Feedback
Refreshment break
Second Clip
Whole group and small group work
Feedback
Closing worship
Questions for personal reflection

It is envisaged the the session takes place in the context of prayer and worship. A Bible text is offered for reading at the beginning, which can then lead into an opening prayer committing the evening to God. Readers are needed for the closing liturgies and space for extempory prayer is given, with suggested subjects for prayer related to each session's theme.

If meeting in person thought must be given to refreshments – who will organise it, will there be a rota, who will bring the milk and biscuits?

The job of the leader or leaders is to facilitate, not to dominate the meetings. They do not need to be the fount of all knowledge, holding the definitive answers. If a leader does not know the answer to someone's direct question, they should be honest and say so, and not try to wing it. If need be, they can say that they will try to find an answer for next time.

For best results groups need to foster a genuine sense of community where consideration and respect for others is important. When confidentiality is practised by all participants, a safe place for sharing personal thoughts and beliefs can be created. Such an environment establishes trust that will bond groups together, nurturing the ground for a rich exploration of the issues raised.

The leader should draw attention to the group guidelines offered below and agree them with the members from the start. Other ground rules can be added with everyone's agreement. It may be worth reminding the group of these commitments from time to time.

Ensure that everyone has the opportunity to speak but does not feel pressured to do so. Quieter group members may need encouragement, more vocal members may need gentle reminders to leave space for others and not dominate the conversation. All participants should be affirmed as members of the course whose views should be heard.

Try to mix up groups so that the same people are not always together. Avoid having couples in the same small group, initially at any rate.

At small group feedback times dissuade reporting that identifies individual opinions ('In our group, Jane said…'), this may be breaking a confidence established in the small group.

Also try to keep feedback brief – headline news not a verbatim report is what is needed.

The leader needs to keep a firm eye on the clock, drawing conversations to a close when needed in order to keep things on track.

Don't forget to set up the second clip during the refreshment break to avoid unnecessary delay.

If all has gone well and it has been fun, members may want to meet again, perhaps after Easter to consider some aspects of the course in greater detail or to take a look at the Postscript.

Who knows, maybe a new homegroup will be born!

Group Guidelines

It is advisable to agree some behaviour guidelines among yourselves to ensure respect and consideration of others:

(1) Be a good listener: try to learn from what others have to say

(2) Do not fear silences: give others room to think and to have their say

(3) Share only what you are comfortable sharing

(4) Resist the urge to correct others, be respectful of their views

(5) Respect confidentiality: outside the group do not discuss individual participants

(6) Commit to doing the Preparatory Reading before each meeting

Other guidelines the group agree to adopt...

If meeting on Zoom

Many of us are familiar with the joys and challenges of Zoom! It is well established that Zoom meetings can be exhausting due to the lack of the non-verbal cues we usually rely on, and the frustrations encountered when delays on the line make responses seem cool or unfriendly. It can therefore be difficult to relax into the kind of conversations we enjoy when meeting face to face. Therefore, to ease the way as much as possible please try to observe the following additional guidelines:

( ) Ensure that your face can be clearly seen when speaking – this will aid understanding

( ) Mute your microphone when film clips are being shown – to reduce background noise

3

The Course

Week One: Setting Out
Preparatory Reading

Abraham had faith and obeyed God. He was told to go to the land that God had said would be his, and he left for a country he had never seen.
Hebrews 11.8 (CEV)

As we prepare to follow Ramanujan's story from his home in India to a new life in a foreign land, we begin by reflecting on our own experience of home: what did your first home mean to you, what were its benefits and its drawbacks, what was it like to leave home for the first time, and what does home mean to you today?

In Kenneth Grahame's *The Wind in the Willows*, Mole and Rat are returning from a winter walk when Mole suddenly catches the scent of his old home on the air, stopping him in his tracks. Overcome with a desire to see it again, Mole pleads with his friend:

> 'You don't understand! It's my home, my old home! I've just come across the smell of it, and it's close by here, really quite close. And I *must* go to it, I must, I must! O, come back, Ratty! Please, please come back' (Grahame, 1908: 86).

All home-loving people will empathise with Mole. For them, home is a place of refuge; the safe place to be oneself; where warmth, acceptance, and a sense of belonging are found.

Sadly, not everyone's home is so positive: many live with

poor housing conditions, or in impoverished circumstances; others must cope with overcrowding; others with the fear of abuse and physical violence. Anyone who does not have a safe home to return to will know isolation and loneliness. Homelessness is now a major problem in the UK, one of the world's richest countries: the charity Crisis UK estimates that the homeless numbers exceeded 200,000 in 2020, just prior to the pandemic. Much homelessness is invisible to the eye for it includes those secretly bedding down in sheds and garages, those who are sofa surfing in friends' homes, and those who spend time in temporary hostels or Bed and Breakfast accommodation. The causes of homelessness are complex and often reflect other vulnerabilities related to health, justice or access to social services. A homeless person is far more likely to take their own life than are members of the general population. Habitat for Humanity (USA) reports that finding secure places for the homeless; a stable home to call their own, makes just about everything else possible: hope and a worthwhile future.

In the opening scenes of our film, we glimpse Ramanujan at home in India with his young wife and elderly mother. Despite the obvious tensions, it is a loving and safe environment in which he can be himself. His love of mathematics threatens to take him away from that home to a place where his talent can be recognised and supported. But there is a problem: Brahmin are not permitted to cross the oceans. To travel to Europe would threaten him with being seen as polluted by the world and therefore in danger of being excluded from his caste. Although the film doesn't show it, Ramanujan at first turns down Hardy's invitation to join him, much to the academic's dismay. What was it that eventually changed Ramanujan's mind? Accounts differ. Hardy would remember that Professor Eric Neville, a fellow of Trinity, was luckily lecturing in Madras at the time and managed to persuade the mother to give her consent to the trip. Sources in India say the goddess Namagiri came to the rescue: she gave her permission in a dream – either directly to Ramanujan or through his mother. The trip was then made possible by grants from both Trinity College, Cambridge, and the University of Madras.

The leaving of home to set out on a perilous quest is a plotline we are all very familiar with. For example, in literature we have Homer's *Odyssey*, Bunyan's *Pilgrim's Progress*, and Tolkien's *The Lord of the Rings*. From the cinema we can cite Victor Fleming's *The Wizard of Oz* (1939) and Steven Spielberg's *Raiders of the Lost Ark* (1981). Setting out on a journey to an unknown land to face daunting challenges takes courage and conviction, as well as requiring painful sacrifices; the film reimagines some of the hardships that Ramanujan suffered.

The Bible is also full of characters who experienced the cost of leaving the security of home to make a necessary journey into the unknown. Early on in Genesis we are introduced to a figure who is central to the whole biblical story, the man of faith, Abram, later renamed Abraham. He was willing to leave his home in Ur (Iraq) in an unquestioning response to God's call:

'Go from your country and your kindred and your father's house to the land that I will show you. I will make of you a great nation, and I will bless you, and make your name great, so that you will be a blessing. I will bless those who bless you, and the one who curses you I will curse; and in you all the families of the earth shall be blessed' (Genesis 12.1–3).

The promise to bless Abram with many descendants is repeated three more times:

'I will make your offspring like the dust of the earth; so that if one can count the dust of the earth, your offspring also can be counted' (Genesis 13.16).

'Look towards heaven and count the stars, if you are able to count them.' Then he said to him, 'So shall your descendants be' (Genesis 15.5).

'No longer shall your name be Abram, but your name shall be Abraham; for I have made you the ancestor of a multitude of nations' (Genesis 17.5).

Abraham was an old man, and his wife was past childbearing, but Abraham took God at his word, trusting that the promise would be fulfilled. Scripture says: 'He believed the LORD; and the LORD reckoned it to him as righteousness' (Genesis 15.6). Abraham set out, not knowing where he was going or what lay in store for him, to become a stranger in a foreign land. Walking by faith and not by sight he became the model for all who set out on the adventure of trusting God's promises.

In the New Testament the incarnation of Jesus Christ is the supreme example of leaving home to face challenges and trials in order to achieve a great purpose. Every Christmas we hear the words of the prologue to St John's gospel:

'He came to what was his own, and his own people did not accept him. But to all who received him, who believed in his name, he gave power to become children of God, who were born, not of blood or of the will of the flesh or of the will of man, but of God. And the Word became flesh and lived among us, and we have seen his glory, the glory as of a father's only son, full of grace and truth' (John 1.10–14).

This is one of the great doctrines of the church; all Christians respond in thanksgiving, worship, and praise in the knowledge of Christ coming amongst us as a child born of Mary, for our sake. St Paul quotes a very early hymn or credal statement in one of his letters:

'[T]hough he was in the form of God, did not regard equality with God as something to be exploited, but emptied himself, taking the form of a slave, being born in human likeness. And being found in human form, he humbled himself and became obedient to the point of death – even death on a cross' (Philippians 2.6–8).

Today there are many wonderful hymns and carols celebrating Christ's incarnation, giving voice to its profound riches. One is the much-loved hymn of Emily Elizabeth Steele Elliott (1836–97) which begins:

Thou didst leave Thy throne
and Thy kingly crown,
when Thou camest to earth for me.

It goes on to speak of Christ's humility in coming to earth, his sufferings, rejection and death, before a final great victory. For this to be the case the New Testament is adamant that Jesus was both fully human and fully God. The gospels show us clearly the humanity of Jesus of Nazareth. Although his conception was indeed unique, he otherwise underwent the normal processes of human birth, growth and development, into full adulthood. Matthew's gospel presents us with Jesus' family tree, his forebears traced back through the line of David, to the patriarch Abraham. Luke's gospel goes even further, tracking Jesus' line all the way to Adam, the first human being. The full array of human experiences and emotions are shown to be his: he is limited in his knowledge; he has compassion for fellow human beings and love for his friends; he can be surprised, frustrated, weary, and in tears; his suffers agonising pain, and knows desolation before death. Yet the gospels also see him as someone who is more than we are: he can calm the wind and waves; he can heal the sick and raise the dead; he has authority to forgive the sins of others; he prays to his Father in heaven in ways that show the closest familial relationship; and he, himself, is sinless.

In a short time after the crucifixion, Jesus' resurrection from the dead was being proclaimed. The New Testament writers were saying that Jesus Christ had been exalted to the right hand of God; he was Saviour of the world but also the creator of the universe; equal with God and therefore worthy of our worship. 'Jesus is Lord' is proclaimed courageously within the Roman Empire, where before only Caesar claimed that title. In the next few centuries, the Church had to come to terms with the implications of all this, the result being the doctrine of the Holy Trinity. For example, the Athanasian Creed (fifth century) affirms God as Father and Son and Holy Spirit, three co-equal 'persons' of the one God, equally divine and uncreated, and all co-operating in every divine act.

It is important to say that the doctrine of the Holy Trinity was not invented by the Church, but that it was waiting to be realised, for it was the inevitable consequence of the Christian experience of God: God is the one who raised Jesus Christ from the dead, and who is now present to us through the Holy Spirit. The Trinity is not a conundrum to be solved or explained away on Trinity Sunday, but the ultimate reality to be encountered. The moment we try to split apart the three persons we will be distorting the truth. God the Father does not act independently of God the Son or of God the Holy Spirit; rather God is always experienced as Trinity in Unity.

So, for example, when it comes to looking at the cross it is important not to split the three persons of the Godhead apart, but to see its work as 'the self-substitution of God', for our sake. We should not speak of God punishing Jesus on the cross, or of Jesus persuading God to accept his sacrifice. To do this would be to give the impression that they act as independent agents, capable of conflicting with each other. It was God in Christ, who was uniquely qualified to mediate on our behalf, because he was both fully God and fully human. Therefore, the fundamental importance of the incarnation of Jesus cannot be overestimated in Christian theology.

Before the first meeting, spend some time reflecting on what home means to you. Think of a time when you left home to embark on a new chapter of your life. How did it feel? Ponder Christ's lowly birth. What was he giving up? How have you experienced God the Holy Trinity: God beyond us, God beside us, God within us?

The Meeting
Welcome and Group Introductions

Opening worship
Read Genesis 12.1,2 *Go from your country and your kindred...*

Leader's Input
A brief recap of the two central characters: Srinivasa Ramanujan and G.H. Hardy (see Part 1).

What does home mean to you?

Notes about this session's film clips:
(i)   Chief Characters
      Madras
      Ramanujan
      Janaki, his wife
      Ramanujan's mother
      Cambridge
      G. H. Hardy
      John Littlewood

(ii)   Hardy's servant refers to 'Gunga Din' the subject of Rudyard Kipling's poem, set in British India:

'Of all them blackfaced crew
The finest man I knew
Was our regimental bhisti [*watercarrier*], Gunga Din,
He was 'Din! Din! Din!'
(Kipling 1890)

(iii) The newspaper headline: 'Austrian Heir and wife murdered' – the shooting of Archduke Ferdinand in Sarajevo in June, 1914, which sparked the events leading to the first world war. (The film delays Ramanujan's arrival by two and a half months.)

Film Clip 1: 11.56–19.29 [7.33] *Ramanujan with his mother – on the beach with Janaki*

First thoughts: What are your first impressions of this clip?

Small group work
1. What memories do you have of leaving home and going to something new? How did it feel?
2. We have already mentioned Abraham, what other Bible characters left home? What were their reasons?
3. Read Luke 5.1–11 *Fishermen leave their nets and follow Jesus*. What were they leaving behind? What motivated them to go?

Feedback to the whole group

Refreshments

Film Clip 2: 19.29–26.09 [6.40] *Cutting hair – Come along, come along*

First thoughts: What are your first impressions of this clip?

Whole Group Discussion

1. What moments stood out for you in this clip?
2. How are the fellows at Trinity portrayed?
3. What impressions are you getting of Hardy's and Littlewood's characters?

Small group work

1. What kinds of sacrifices were Ramanujan and Janaki making?
2. How do you imagine Ramanujan feels as he is received into the common room at Trinity?
3. What situations in our own lives might make us experience something of the same feelings?
4. In the film Hardy tells his colleagues that change is a wonderful thing that should be embraced. Do you agree with him? Why/Why not?
5. Read John 1.14, John 3.16,17 and Philippians 2.5–11. In the context of leaving home and entering a different culture, how do these texts speak to you of Christ's Incarnation?

Feedback to the whole group

Closing worship

Christ has called us out of darkness
to dwell in his marvellous light. *(cf 1 Peter 2.9)*

Galatians 4.4,5
But when the right time finally came, God sent his own Son. He came as the son of a human mother and lived under the Jewish Law, to redeem those who were under the Law, so that we might become God's children (CEV).

1 John 1.1–4

That which was from the beginning, which we have heard, which we have seen with our eyes, which we have looked at and our hands have touched – this we proclaim concerning the Word of life. The life appeared; we have seen it and testify to it, and we proclaim to you the eternal life, which was with the Father and has appeared to us. We proclaim to you what we have seen and heard, so that you also may have fellowship with us. And our fellowship is with the Father and with his Son, Jesus Christ. We write this to make our joy complete (NIV).

> Lord Jesus Christ,
> **we bring you our thanks and praise**
> because in your incarnation
> **a new light has dawned upon us;**
> the true light which gives light to all
> **that we might become children of God**
> **to the Father's glory.** *(cf John 1.4,12)*
> **Amen.**

Prayers may be offered:
- *for those leaving home and journeying into new situations*
- *for those facing change, wanted or unwanted*
- *for those hearing the call of God to step out in faith and take on fresh challenges*

Blessed are those whose strength is in you,
whose hearts are set on pilgrimage. *(Psalm 84.5 (NIV))*
Lord, we will trust You,
in You we put our hope.
As we journey together on this course
help us to step out in faith
to question old assumptions
and explore new possibilities.

May the peace of God
which transcends all understanding
guard our hearts and our minds
in Christ Jesus our Lord. *(cf Philippians 4.7)*

In the name of the Father,
and of the Son,
and of the Holy Spirit.
Amen.

Questions for personal reflection

1. How did the Covid-19 restrictions make me feel differently about home?
2. Why is it so important that Jesus was both fully human and fully divine?
3. What inspires me to be a follower of Jesus Christ?
4. Have I the courage to leave the familiar and journey into the unknown?

Personal Notes...

Week Two: Life in a foreign land
Preparatory Reading

How could we sing the Lord's song in a foreign land?
Psalm 137.4

In this session we look at how the film imagines Ramanujan's first days at Trinity College in 1914 and his first taste of exile. When we think of exiles what may first come to mind is someone like Napoleon who was banished, for political reasons, to live out the rest of his days on St Helena, or the Dalai Lama fleeing Tibet for a life in India, or Soviet dissidents languishing in the Siberian Gulags. None of them chose their destinations any more than those forced into Nazi concentration camps or Chinese 're-education' centres. In his book *Praying in Exile,* Gordon Mursell offers a wider definition, he says exile is: 'any situation or experience in which you are not at home, and not in control of what is happening to you' (Mursell 2005:1,2). Tax exiles do not fit this definition, but refugees from war, famine, climate change or ethnic cleansing certainly do. They must learn to cope in foreign lands where the language and culture may be different, and the people may not want them. Ramanujan was not compelled to leave India, but he was faced with the challenge of not being 'at home', of not being in control of what was happening, and of needing to cope with the disapproval and mistrust of many around him. Gordon Mursell's definition can be helpful in understanding our own spiritual lives too, perhaps not least when having to learn how to cope with the isolation caused by Covid-19.

   The Coronavirus pandemic has been a humanitarian calamity. Many of the world's hospitals have been overwhelmed to the point of collapse, as the death toll has soared to many millions worldwide. Countries have been forced into lockdowns, seen businesses ruined, jobs lost, and normal social interactions suspended, as infection rates have run out of control. In the UK, the situation for its care homes has been particularly tragic. At the best of times life in a care home means loss of independence, but when physical frailty, the loss of hearing, or the onset of dementia become acute, the sense of isolation becomes intense. The lockdown measures of 2020–21 saw residents quarantined in their rooms for months on end, unable to receive family visits – even, in the saddest cases, during the final hours of life. In addition to personal family tragedies, this country's high death toll has had its impact on all care home staff, hospital nurses, doctors and health workers, affecting their own health and wellbeing. The discovery of the vaccines and their speedy roll-out has been a scientific and medical triumph, but we still live with the threat of new variants and the possibility of further disruptive measures.

If exile is never feeling fully at home, then it must describe something of our spiritual lives as well. St Augustine famously prayed to God: 'We are restless till we find our rest in you.' There is a restlessness in the human heart that nothing physical can satisfy. It is a nagging feeling that something is not right, something is missing; we keep looking for the missing ingredient in the wrong places, for example, in money, sex, or power. Ultimately, these things don't satisfy. The longing remains and we still feel alienated and exiled. Whether we recognise it or not, that restlessness is a God-shaped hole within us that only God can fill. In the language we are using in this course that equates to exile: a longing for home, our true home in God.

It is very striking just how often the theme of exile occurs in the Bible. Here are just four examples: firstly, we have Adam and Eve, banished from their home in the Garden of Eden through their disobedience of God; then there is Jacob fleeing from Esau after stealing his brother's birthright; another is Joseph, whose jealous brothers sell him into slavery in Egypt, leading eventually to all the Israelite tribes being in bondage there, before God moves to free them to settle, one day, in their promised land. My fourth example occurs many centuries later, when the Jews are exiled to Babylon following that country's destruction of Jerusalem and its Temple in 587 BC. Jeremiah had anticipated this crisis, but he had gone unheeded. But now, amid their pain and humiliation, the Jews struggled with some big questions: why had God allowed this disaster to happen, what now of his promises to them, was there any hope of returning home? The inescapable conclusion was that the people of the promise were not immune from the consequence of their sin; estrangement from God (exile in Babylon) was the inevitable penalty for their failure to be faithful to him.

The exile was to last 70 years, towards the end of which, God spoke through the prophet Isaiah these consoling words:

Comfort, O comfort my people,
says your God.
Speak tenderly to Jerusalem,
and cry to her
that she has served her term,
that her penalty is paid,
that she has received from the Lord's hand
double for all her sins (Isaiah 40.1,2).

The people finally returned and rebuilt their city and its Temple, but nothing really changed. There remained the feeling that their separation from God had not really ended, the exile was not over. Indeed, estrangement from God was not only Israel's problem. The exile became a metaphor for universal human sinfulness, separating us from God and our true home in him. Again, it was the prophet Isaiah who recognised that humanity's exile would never be over until one final, shocking exile had taken place. In one of the so-called Servant Songs Isaiah writes:

Surely he has borne our infirmities
and carried our diseases;
yet we accounted him stricken,
struck down by God, and afflicted.
But he was wounded for our transgressions,
crushed for our iniquities;
upon him was the punishment that made us whole,
and by his bruises we are healed.
All we like sheep have gone astray;
we have all turned to our own way,
and the Lord has laid on him
the iniquity of us all (Isaiah 53.4–6).

The Servant Songs imagine a figure cast away just like Israel had been in Babylon. This Servant would be overwhelmed with shame and suffering and death – 'cut off from the land of the living, stricken for the transgression of my people' (53.8). However, there would also be a final vindication, 'he shall see his offspring, and shall prolong his days ... I will allot him a portion with the great, and he shall divide the spoil with the strong' (53.10,12). But who would be this mysterious Servant figure? Was Isaiah looking to the whole nation of Israel to fulfil that role, or was it to be one individual Israelite, a true and faithful servant of God?

To the earliest Christians, Isaiah's words spoke loudly and clearly of Jesus. He had been *the* Servant King who laid down his life for them. The one who had enjoyed the closest possible relationship with the Father, had now suffered the humiliation and dereliction of the Roman cross, and plumbed the full meaning of its exile: 'My God, my God, why have you forsaken me?' (Mark 15.34). Suffering and dying he had risen again triumphant over death, the vindicated Son of God bringing forgiveness, restoration, and the promise of new life. In the cross, St Paul saw that it was God himself, in the person of Jesus

Christ, who was reconciling the world to himself (2 Corinthians 5.19); God embracing exile for us all, in order that we might be freed from it and brought home.

Israel had lost its way, looked for home in all the wrong places. They had wanted warrior kings, and ultimately a Messiah, to bring them freedom and peace. But Jesus refused to go the way of violence; he was the one true Israelite, who walked the path of sacrificial love, forgiveness, and the welcome of the outsider. Jesus said: 'I am the way, and the truth, and the life. No one comes to the Father except through me' (John 14.6). Jesus is the way out of all our spiritual exiles, he is the road home to God.

The Christian writer of the Letter to the Hebrews spoke of all followers of Jesus being strangers and foreigners on the earth, journeying to another homeland. Speaking of the great examples of faith in the past the writer says:

'If they had been thinking of the land that they had left behind, they would have had opportunity to return. But as it is, they desire a better country, that is, a heavenly one. Therefore God is not ashamed to be called their God; indeed, he has prepared a city for them' (Hebrews 11. 15,16).

Interestingly, our true home is not pictured as a return to a garden in Eden, but as a new destination: a new Jerusalem, a city of many dwellings where God will dwell with his people and 'wipe every tear from their eyes' (Revelation 21.4). Until then, Jesus' people must learn to live Christ-like lives in exile from this glorious home, with all the challenges that will bring them. Such a life of faith will require learning to let go and trust God.

Before the meeting, reflect on what living in exile, 'out of control', can mean for a follower of Jesus Christ.

The Meeting

Opening worship
Read Hebrews 11.13–16 *Strangers and Foreigners on earth*

Recap of last week: Setting Out
Ramanujan leaves India and journeys to Cambridge in 1914. His reception at Trinity College is against a background of approaching war.
Any further thoughts or questions from last week?

This week: Life in a Foreign Land

Whole Group Discussion
1. Using the definition that exile is any situation or experience in which someone is not at home, and not in control of what is happening to them, who are the exiles of today?
2. Describe a time when you have felt 'not at home' or 'not in control'.

Notes about this session's film clips:
Additional characters:
Chandra: Trinity student from India
Andrew: Trinity student from England
Bertie: Bertrand Russell – Fellow; philosopher and pacifist
Mr Howard: Mathematics Fellow, aggressive critic of Ramanujan's presence in the College

Film Clip 1: 26.09–33.06 [6.57] *Ramanujan's study – I'll say goodnight then.*

First thoughts: What are your first impressions of this clip?

Whole Group Discussion

1. List some of the ways that the film conveys the strange and uncomfortable environment Ramanujan has entered.
2. What spiritual resources do Christians have for coping with isolation and not being able to meet up with others for worship?
3. Ramanujan was a strict vegetarian, but vegetarianism was little known in England in 1914 and Hardy shows no understanding of the challenges his new student faces. Why might Ramanujan be reluctant to alert the College to his dietary needs? (It is going to have a big effect on Ramanujan's health.)

Small Group Work

1. Read Psalm 137 composed during the Babylonian Exile. The psalmist's lament gives voice to complaint, implicitly questions God, and even expresses fierce anger. How comfortable do you feel using such words in your own private prayer and in public worship?
2. Here are three texts about welcoming strangers:
   - 'When an alien resides with you in your land, you shall not oppress the alien. The alien who resides with you shall be to you as the citizen among you; you shall love the alien as yourself, for you were aliens in the land of Egypt: I am the Lord your God' (Leviticus 19.33,34).
   - 'The Lord watches over the strangers; he upholds the orphan and the widow, but the way of the wicked he brings to ruin' (Psalm 146.9).
   - 'Let mutual love continue. Do not neglect to show hospitality to strangers, for by doing that some have entertained angels without knowing it' (Hebrews 13.1,2).

How would you describe God's attitude to strangers and aliens?

Feedback to the whole group

Refreshments

Film Clip 2: 33.06–34.59 [3.57] *Mr Howard's lecture – A little humility would go a long way*

First thoughts: What are your first impressions of this clip?

Small Group Work

1. Mr Howard tries to humiliate Ramanujan in front of the other students and then abuses him racially. Where does discrimination (race, gender or class) operate in the Church today?

2. Anger can quickly be followed by contempt and easily results in violence. When is it right to be angry and when isn't it? Is contempt (the act or mental attitude of despising another person) ever acceptable?

3. Read Ephesians 4.1–6. The film paints a picture of a college community that is highly competitive, intellectually elitist, and in part racist. In contrast to that, a church that is truly alive in the Spirit will be one in which all racial, cultural, social, and educational barriers are eliminated. Make a list of the kind of changes a church might need to make to nurture 'unity of the Spirit in the bond of peace'.

Feedback to the whole group

Closing worship
O God, make speed to save us.
O Lord, make haste to help us.

My trust is in you, O Lord.
I have said, 'You are my God'. *(Psalm 31.14 (NIV))*

1 Peter 2.23–25

When he was abused, he did not return abuse; when he suffered, he did not threaten; but he entrusted himself to the one who judges justly. He himself bore our sins in his body on the cross, so that, free from sins, we might live for righteousness; by his wounds you have been healed. For you were going astray like sheep, but now you have returned to the shepherd and guardian of your souls.

Prayers may be offered:
- *for those in any kind of exile*
- *for those oppressed or persecuted*
- *for those who feel they are alone*

O Lord, you have searched me and known me.
You know when I sit down and when I rise up;
you discern my thoughts from far away.
Even before a word is on my tongue,
you know it completely.
You hem me in, behind and before,
and lay your hand upon me.

Where can I go from your spirit?
Or where can I flee from your presence?
If I ascend to heaven,
you are there;
if I make my bed in Sheol,
you are there.
If I take the wings of the morning
and settle at the farthest limits of the sea,
you are there.
Your hand shall guide me,
your right hand will hold me fast. (*cf Psalm 139 (NIV)*)
May Christ our Saviour give us peace.

Amen.

Questions for personal reflection

1. What are the pros and the cons about feeling at home in a church?

2. According to Jesus' parable of the sheep and the goats (Matthew 25), every human encounter is a possible meeting with him. How should that affect my attitude and behaviour towards strangers, especially the least?

3. Why is it so difficult to let go and trust God?

4. In Week One we considered the problems of seeing the cross as God punishing Jesus or Jesus persuading God. How do I understand the cross?

Personal Notes...

Week Three: What is truth?
Preparatory Reading

The fear of the Lord is the beginning of wisdom.
Proverbs 9.10

In Charles Dickens' novel *Hard Times* the School Board Superintendent, Mr Thomas Gradgrind, is not interested in anything but facts, reminding the teacher:

'Now, what I want is, Facts. Teach these boys and girls nothing but Facts. Facts alone are wanted in life. Plant nothing else, and root out everything else. You can only form the minds of reasoning animals upon Facts: nothing else will ever be of any service to them. This is the principle on which I bring up my own children, and this is the principle on which I bring up these children. Stick to Facts, sir!' (Dickens, 1854:9).

The teacher is Mr M'Choakumchild, who squeezes out of his charges any room for imagination or appreciation of beauty. Such cold rationality values only 'objective facts' and relegates everything else to worthless opinion. Today this level of rationalism can exclude religious belief as well. Richard Dawkins' critique of religion is well known through his books such as *The God Delusion* and his public debates, where he claims that there is no evidence for the divine and that all real scientists should be atheists. He and other advocates of the 'new atheism' describe all faith as blind faith, devoid of any supporting evidence; it can be used to justify anything, making it both irrational and dangerous.

The Oxford English Dictionary defines faith as 'reliance or trust in', and a moment's thought will convince us that faith is therefore an everyday necessity: we all exercise faith whenever we develop a friendship, undergo a medical procedure, deposit our money in the bank, or get on an aeroplane. To claim that science does not require faith is a grave distortion. To proceed at all scientists must take certain things on trust; most fundamentally that the world has a rational, intelligible nature which conforms to certain laws. This is an act of faith not a fact, but without it, science would be impossible, having no ground to stand on. Science is also often portrayed as being purely objective in its methods, built only on detached observation and experiment, but it is a very human enterprise, sometimes requiring its practitioners to think out of the box, to use their intuition and imagination to create new theories worthy of testing. People may say that doubt is always the safest position to take, more honest than faith, but even atheism has its beliefs, built on the conviction that God does not exist. When it comes to the Christian faith, none of us would advocate blind trust, rather we will say that our faith is based on good, persuasive evidence.

Where does knowledge come from and how do we *know* something is true? This is the province of an area of philosophy called epistemology (Greek *epistēmē* meaning knowledge). In our postmodern culture many people are quite happy to say things like: 'That might be true for you, but it is not true for me', in other words, there is no such thing as an objective truth: all truth is relative. However, others will argue: 'no, if something is true, then it must be universally true'. There is an obvious tension between those who wish to reduce all truth to facts, like Mr Gradgrind, and those who see truth in a more relational and inclusive way. This is not simply an academic matter, it affects how we understand the world, relate to one another, and order our societies. Clearly, truth matters.

Is truth only that which can be proved with mathematical certainty or reduced to facts like 'Paris is the capital of France'? Surely there are other truths which are not contained in these categories. Not even the most complete rationalist would say that there is no truth in human love. In the Bible truth is more than about being correct rather than in error; it involves faithfulness and reliability, the opposite of lies and deception. A truth is not just an accurate statement, it can be something worthy of personal commitment: truth is what we see when we see God.

There is the kind of relational truth that is central to human life: the knowledge of persons. You cannot prove it mathematically or inspect it scientifically; it can only be known through experience. To come to know another person requires a degree of risky vulnerability: we must begin to trust the other, spend time with them sharing our thoughts, our hopes and even our dreams. We have little control over this way of knowing, because it is about developing a two-way relationship, a friendship, that must be based on faith in the other person, on trust and on love.

It may be true that we can learn something of God through observation of the world he has created (this is called Natural Theology), but such study can only take us so far. For the Christian, the ultimate level of knowing comes through revelation, most strikingly in the incarnation of Jesus Christ, opening up to us the offer of a relationship with the divine. By God's grace we are drawn into relationship with him. To come fully into that truth requires not rational argument, but personal response. When Jesus is summoned to stand before Pontius Pilate and says that he came into the world to testify to the truth, Pilate's response is cynical: 'What is truth?' (John 18.38), and his subsequent actions reveal his lack of concern for it. The tragedy of Pilate's life was his inability or his unwillingness to see the truth of who stood before him: God in human flesh, calling him, and us, into relationship with him.

Last session we spoke of the restlessness that lies within the human heart. We often sense a passion within us for something that is beyond us, greater than us and prior to us. Such feelings may be the result of a desire to see justice done; it might be an appreciation of beauty; or it might be an urge for greater spiritual meaning. These and other promptings are difficult to quantify or to take a firm hold of. Yet such thoughts are like persistent voices that seem to come from beyond us, contributing to our sense of incompleteness, and sending us on a search for deeper contentment.

Our restlessness often results in us searching for completeness in the wrong places, but, if it is a God-given longing, then it is a search for truth. Jesus said to Pilate: 'Everyone who belongs to the truth listens to my voice' (John 18.37). Many of Jesus' wider circle of disciples came to find his teaching too difficult and turned back, so Jesus asked the twelve, 'Do you also wish to go away?' Simon Peter answered him, 'Lord, to whom can we go? You have the words of eternal life' (John 6.68). Towards the end of *Hard Times,* Thomas Gradgrind recognises the tragic consequences that his extreme rationalism has had upon his own children; he laments: 'The ground on which I stand has ceased to be solid under my feet' (Dickens, 1854: 216). From that moment he determines to refocus his life on faith, hope and love.

Christian faith requires a commitment to Christ; a reliance or trust in the person of Jesus who said: 'I am the way, and the truth, and the life' (John 14.6). This faith is exercised in the face of objective uncertainty, to say otherwise would demand a redefinition of the word faith. We do not claim to have any monopoly on truth, in this life there is always more to learn and there will always be grounds for doubt and uncertainty. Truth is often learned the hard way, through painful personal experience.

Set into the floor of the Chapel of St Katherine's Retreat Centre, near Canary Wharf in East London, is a depiction in granite of a large maritime compass. This mosaic has inscribed around it some words attributed to St Augustine: 'We come to

God not by navigation, but by love'. It is a delusion to imagine we can navigate our way through to a fulfilled life via objective truths alone; the open secret is that we can trust the love of Jesus to lead us into the fulness of the truth.

In preparation for the meeting ask yourself why people think it's so important to get to the truth of events like the Hillsborough disaster, the Grenfell fire, George Floyd's death, or the handling of the Covid-19 pandemic. Think about the different sources of knowledge that you have and how you judge things to be true. Think about your own faith and what it is based on.

The Meeting

Opening worship
Read John 8.31,32 *You will know the truth and the truth will make you free.*

Recap of last week: Life in a Foreign Land
To be an exile is to be 'not at home' or 'not in control': a stranger or outsider. Beginning with Ramanujan's experience of life in Cambridge, we considered God's attitude to strangers and aliens; our own attitudes about anger and contempt; Christ the suffering servant sent into exile.

Any further thoughts or questions from last week?

This week: What is truth?
The US Secretary of Defense, Donald Rumsfeld, once famously remarked that there are things we know we know, things we know we don't know, and things we don't know we don't know.

This week we will be asking ourselves:
- Where do we get our knowledge from?
- How do we know that something is true?
- How do we distinguish between justified belief and opinion?

and we will be looking at faith, doubt and certainty.

Notes about moments in today's first film clip:

(i) Hardy has required Ramanujan to attend Mr Howard's mathematics lectures, because he lacks an appreciation for rigorous proof. Last time we left Ramanujan in some distress, having been racially and physically abused by his lecturer.

(ii) Ramanujan is working on something called 'Partitions': for example, how many ways can you make 4 using whole numbers? The answer is 5 or $P(4) = 5$ because $1+1+1+1$, or $3+1$, or $2+1+1$, or $2+2$, or 4, all make 4. The number of ways get very large, very quickly: for example, $P(100) = 204{,}226$

(iii) Now the war has started, Trinity College houses a military hospital, hence the marquees.

(iv) There are references to something called 'the Wren': the library at Trinity College.

Film Clip 1: 40.05–47.05 [7.00] *Ramanujan leaves the P.O. – Thank you, Sir!*

First thoughts: What are your first impressions of this clip?

Whole Group Discussion

In the opening scene we get a glimpse of how Ramanujan believes he gets his knowledge – his god, Namagiri, tells him (i.e., by revelation). In what follows we see a prickly relationship developing between the two men as Hardy demands logical, mathematical proof, and disdains Ramanujan's claim of self-evident rightness. The tension continues in the courtyard: 'I don't think about these things the same way you do....'

1   What sorts of ways of knowing are there? Perhaps the following statements will help:

a) 'I know how to drive a car.'

b) 'I know my way round London.'

c) 'I know that 5 x 5 = 25.'

d) 'I know my wife loves me.'

e) 'The Mona Lisa is a work of great beauty.'

f) 'I hear it's raining outside.'

g) 'I just knew that Jane would call today.'

h) 'I know that my Redeemer liveth.'

2   Is it ever possible to exercise faith without being in the presence of uncertainty?

3   The words 'faith', 'doubt' and 'certainty' have various interpretations, depending on the context they are used in. Certainty can indicate firm faith, but it can also imply a closed mind, an unwillingness to explore new ideas. When believers refuse to explore their convictions or question their actions, are they exercising blind faith?

4   Doubt has a negative press in many Christian circles. Yes, Jesus rebukes Peter: 'You of little faith, why did you doubt?' (Matthew 14.31), but isn't doubt sometimes a necessary and healthy approach if we are to avoid being gullible? Can doubt be positive, stimulating fresh thought, leading to important correctives and sometimes new discoveries?

5   'To have faith is to be sure of the things we hope for, to be certain of the things we cannot see' (Hebrews 11.1 CEV). How do you understand this verse?

6   There is a world of difference between objective mathematical truth, and the truth which is relational. This second kind of truth requires a personal response. Hardy says that he is an atheist, but Ramanujan rejects that, saying: 'You just don't think God likes you.'
In your experience what prevents people from believing in God? How would you answer someone who says of your faith, 'That may be true for you, but not for me.'?

Feedback to the whole group

Refreshments

A note about today's second film clip:

   (i) War has brought food shortages which means Ramanujan has difficulty buying the vegetables he needs to live on. Also, he has been beaten up in the street by disgruntled squaddies.

  (ii) Littlewood has been called up into the army and now writes to Hardy from the front.

Film Clip 2: 56.11–1:02.18 [6.07] *From Mr Littlewood, Sir. – Hardy alone by the tent*

First thoughts: What are your first impressions of this clip?

Small Group Work
Littlewood's letter introduces the topic of friendship: 'Every single positive integer is one of his personal friends'.

In the time available address some of the following questions:

1. What qualities need to be present for a true friendship to grow? Make a list.

2. Ramanujan reacts frustratedly when Hardy questions the value of intuition alone and demands proof. This leads to angry outbursts from both men. What are the triggers to each man's anger?

3. Read Matthew 7.1–5. To live it is necessary to make judgements, about people as well as situations. Therefore, how should we interpret Jesus' instruction 'Do not judge'?

4. In the scene the focus moves from knowing about something to being known; Ramanujan accuses Hardy of never really *seeing* him, let alone getting to *know*

him. It is a turning point in the film, as Hardy sees, for the first time, the man behind the mathematics; perhaps a real friendship can now develop. How do we really get to know another person? What are the likely barriers?

5. Jesus prayed to the Father: 'And this is eternal life, that they may know you, the only true God, and Jesus Christ whom you have sent' (John 17.3). How do we get to know God? J. I. Packer lists four analogies that the Bible has for knowing God:

- a son knowing his father
- a wife knowing her husband
- a subject knowing his king
- a sheep knowing its shepherd (Packer, 1973: 35)

Do these analogies help us to see more clearly what it means to know God?

Feedback to the whole group

Closing worship
The Lord is my light
and my salvation. *(Psalm 27.1)*

Teach me your way, O Lord,
that I may walk in your truth. *(Psalm 86.11)*

John 8.12
Jesus spoke to them, saying, 'I am the light of the world. Whoever follows me will never walk in darkness but will have the light of life.'

John 8.31,32
Then Jesus said to the Jews who had believed in him, 'If you

continue in my word, you are truly my disciples; and you will know the truth, and the truth will make you free.'

John 16.13
Jesus said, 'When the Spirit of truth comes, he will guide you into all the truth.'

Your word is a lamp to my feet
and a light to my path. *(Psalm 119.105)*

Prayers may be offered:
- *for those denied the truth*
- *for those who struggle with doubt*
- *for those who are searching for God*

Ask, and it will be given to you;
search, and you will find;
knock, and the door will be opened for you.
For everyone who asks receives,
and everyone who searches finds,
and for everyone who knocks,
the door will be opened. *(Matthew 7.7,8)*
Thanks be to God.

May the peace of God,
which transcends our understanding,
guard your hearts and your minds
in Christ Jesus, our Lord. *(cf Philippians 4.7)*
Amen.

Questions for personal reflection
1. In the last 24 hours what matters have I been required to take on trust?
2. On what evidence do I base my beliefs, for example, in

the resurrection of Jesus Christ?

3. Towards the end of the film Ramanujan says: 'An equation has no meaning to me unless it expresses a thought of God.' And the psalmist wrote 'The heavens are telling the glory of God; and the firmament proclaims his handiwork' (Psalm 19.1). Can we discern things about God in the natural world, in science, or in mathematics?

4. The Anglican communion service has a prayer that begins: 'Almighty God, to whom all hearts are open, all desires known, and from whom no secrets are hidden....' How does it make me feel that God knows me so completely?

Personal Notes...

Week Four: Bridging the Gap
Preparatory Reading

And he was called the friend of God.

James 2.23

Recently I was on the London Underground platform at Bank Station. When the train arrived and the doors opened, I heard a familiar message coming over the public address system: 'Mind the Gap – mind the gap between the train and the platform'. The combination of a straight train carriage and a curved platform edge means that an unavoidable space is created at that station between a train and the platform. An unsuspecting traveller is in danger of stepping into that void and suffering a painful injury, hence the all-important audible warning. Boarding a small ferry is another example of the need for care in crossing from the quayside to the vessel and back again, although usually there is someone on hand to help with the crossing. Dangerous gaps are all too common in other walks of life too, notably in relationships, where go-betweens have crucial roles to play: war zones need peace envoys; trade disputes, arbitrators; broken marriages, counsellors. Go-betweens work to bring reconciliation between estranged parties.

Following the destruction of Coventry Cathedral in 1940, the Cathedral Provost, Richard Howard, made a radio broadcast declaring that when the war was over, we should work with those who had been our enemies 'to build a kinder, more Christ-like world.' Instead of seeking revenge, he said, we should work to bring forgiveness and reconciliation with those who had been responsible. From that came the *Community of the Cross of Nails*, which has laboured to forge links with the bombed cities of Germany, remembering the devastation that our country brought on those cities later in the war, and building new relationships of peace between the two countries.

One way of thinking of the word 'remember' is to put the emphasis on the 're': re-member or put back together, reconcile. At the Cenotaph in London on Remembrance Sunday, 2018, the Royal Family and representatives of Parliament were joined, for the first time, by the President of Germany, Frank Walter Steinmeier, in the act of remembrance to the fallen in two world wars, giving us a most moving demonstration of reconciliation.

Anyone who has tried to bring parties in angry conflict together will know how difficult and costly it can be. David Trimble, the then leader of the Ulster Unionist Party, played a major role in brokering the Good Friday Agreement in 1998. Senator George Mitchell, the United States Special Envoy, also a key figure in the negotiations, observed of Trimble that he had to navigate his way through a minefield of criticism: daily attacks from the unionists on one side for the ground he was conceding, and the nationalists on the other, who were angered by his perceived stubbornness (see Mitchell, 1999).

Bringing warring parties together gets no more costly than when it is God and sinful humanity that need reconciling. St Paul wrote to believers in Rome of Christ's role in reconciling God to his enemies, through his death on the cross: 'Even when we were God's enemies, he made peace with us, because his Son died for us' (Romans 5.10 CEV). Atonement is the word used to describe this act of peace-making, an at-one-ment with God. To the believers in Galatia Paul writes of God's grace enabling sinners to approach him and enter into his blessing now and hereafter:

'When the fullness of time had come, God sent his Son, born of a woman, born under the law, in order to redeem those who were under the law, so that we might receive adoption as children' (Galatians 4.4,5).

Christ came to experience exile so that our own exile from

God can come to an end. The cross is a deep mystery; several metaphors have been devised in order to view it from different perspectives, to help us gain a deeper appreciation of its riches. They include metaphors of a victory over evil; a sacrifice which removes sin; a ransom price paid to free slaves; a courtroom satisfying justice; an act of reconciliation turning enemies into friends. All are important, no one metaphor can give a complete picture, and some images are more accessible today than others. Reconciliation also has a part to play in the Ramanujan – Hardy story. Tom Smail has described the Calvary scene in terms of Jesus being *the* reconciling friend of God, for when God looks at Jesus on the cross, he sees him praying for his enemies, and God's own self-giving love is reflected back to him out of the darkness of sin and death. In forgiving and praying for his enemies, this friend *of* God makes a renewed friendship *with* God possible for all, through our simple trust in his sacrifice. (see Smail, 1995).

The only person in the Bible to be called 'friend of God' is Abraham, who was also involved with a costly sacrifice. In the Letter of James, we read:

'Was not our ancestor Abraham justified by works when he offered his son Isaac on the altar? You see that faith was active along with his works, and faith was brought to completion by the works. Thus the scripture was fulfilled that says, "Abraham believed God, and it was reckoned to him as righteousness", and he was called the friend of God' (James 2.21–25).

This is a reference to Abraham being tested by God to sacrifice his son Isaac on Mount Moriah. Isaac's birth to Abraham and Sarah had been miraculous, because Sarah was well past childbearing age. God had promised this child to Abraham and Sarah, and said that through him Abraham would have more offspring than stars in the sky, and 'in you [that is, in your offspring] all the families of the earth shall be blessed' (Genesis 12.3). Yet in Genesis 22.2 God tells Abraham:

'Take your son, your only son Isaac, whom you love, and go to the land of Moriah, and offer him there as a burnt-offering on one of the mountains that I shall show you.'

Abraham was certainly tested, and although a ram, caught in a thicket, was in the end the actual sacrifice, this passage of scripture is very problematic for many people. The Old Testament makes it plain that God detested child sacrifice (for example, see Leviticus 20.2–5), how then could he tell Abraham to do it?

Commentators ancient and modern have seen it as God simply testing Abraham's obedience, a test he passed with flying colours. That, they say, is the meaning of the story. God had always intended a substitute to be found. However, some will still find the fact that God commanded Abraham to do it in the first place, something that is morally very dubious. Rabbi Jonathan Sacks has offered an additional perspective: Abraham was caught in a contradiction between God's word to him now and God's word on previous occasions. As there was yet no clarifying word, the test could have been not so much one of his obedience, but of his ability to live with uncertainty until further clarification was given (see Sacks, 2019).

Turning again to the film, last week we saw Ramanujan and Hardy quarrelling over the importance of proof and intuition, as Hardy insisted on obtaining absolute certainty of Ramanujan's claims. Ponder Jonathan Sack's take on the testing of Abraham and ask yourself how comfortable you are living with uncertainty.

This week the story moves on to portray the growing friendship that blossoms between the two men of vastly different backgrounds, outlooks and beliefs. Give some thought to the values and the qualities you think are essential to sustain good friendships.

Reflect on Christ's role in reconciling you to God. Do you see Jesus as your friend as well as your Lord and Saviour?

The Meeting

Opening worship:
Read John 3.16 *For God so loved the world...*

Recap of last week: What is Truth?
Where do we get our knowledge from? How do we distinguish between a justified belief and an opinion? What, if anything, is the value of doubt? Is certainty always a good thing? What does it mean to *know* God?

We also started thinking about friendship and what it might mean to know God as our friend.

Any further thoughts or questions from last week?

This week: Bridging the Gap (more about the nature of friendship).

Whole Group Discussion
Reflect on this description of friendship:

'But oh! the blessing it is to have a friend to whom one can speak fearlessly on any subject; with whom one's deepest as well as one's most foolish thoughts come out simply and safely. Oh, the comfort – the inexpressible comfort of feeling *safe* with a person, having neither to weigh thoughts, nor measure words, but pouring them all out, just as they are, chaff and grain together; knowing that a faithful hand will take and sift them – keep what is worth keeping – and with the breath of kindness blow the rest away' (Craik, 1859: 169).

1. How true is it to your experience?
2. Does it in any way reflect your friendship with God?

Notes about moments in today's first film clip:
Additional character:

Major MacMahon: Trinity Fellow; expert on partitions; an aggressive critic of Ramanujan

A challenge is set to calculate P(200). MacMahon embarks on the Herculean task of doing it by hand and gets the exact value: P(200) = 3,972,999,029,388. Ramanujan and Hardy work together (seen here in partnership at the blackboard) to refine a formula to achieve an accurate result – something that was said to be impossible.

Film Clip 1: 1.02.18 – 1.09.10 [6.54] *On the Chapel steps – on the Surgery steps*

First thoughts: What are your first impressions of this clip?

Whole Group Discussion
1. Do you think that Bertie is being fair when he tells Hardy that his treatment of Ramanujan has been too severe?
2. MacMahon does not hide his contempt for Ramanujan and his work, as he looks forward to the spectacular failure of the formula. We all have an unpleasant trait which relishes the misfortune of others (Schadenfreude); why do we delight in putting others down and seeing them fail?

Small Group Work
The Ramanujan formula produced P(200) = 3,972,998,029,388, an amazingly close result for their first attempt – just 1 million out! It was later refined and published, becoming known as The Hardy-Ramanujan Asymptotic Formula. What we are seeing

is two men growing to become true collaborators and friends. MacMahon's contempt for Ramanujan melts away when he sees the formula predict a result remarkably close to the true one; contempt is replaced by respect.

1.   Article 1 of The Universal Declaration of Human Rights states: All human beings are born free and equal in dignity and rights. What are the Christian roots of respect for all?

2.   St Paul wrote: 'Let love be genuine' (Romans 12.9). How can you love someone you don't really like?

3.   How is love depicted in the Gospels?

4.   Why is it so difficult to forgive?

Feedback to the whole group

Refreshments

Notes about moments in today's second film clip:

1.   In the first clip, we saw Ramanujan coughing badly: he is now diagnosed with signs of terminal TB.

2.   Previously Hardy had requested the College to give his friend a Fellowship, but the council refused, this was a great blow to both men.

3.   An important aspect of the film we have not seen is that Ramanujan has not received answers to his many letters to his wife in India, he fears she has forgotten him.

4.   In great distress he attempts suicide by stepping in front of a tube train, but thanks to the alertness of the driver Ramanujan receives only superficial injuries. We pick up the story with Ramanujan in a nursing home.

Film Clip 2: 1.21.04–1.26.55 [5.51] *Are you warm enough? – See this gets to Lt Littlewood*

First thoughts: What are your first impressions of this clip?

Small Group Work

1. Evidence that an honest friendship is growing between them is their mutual vulnerability, as they share something of their personal beliefs. But then Hardy says: 'I don't believe in anything I can't prove,' to which Ramanujan replies: 'Then you can't believe in me.' How is it possible to have a deep friendship with someone of very different beliefs?

2. St Paul writes: 'God put the world square with himself through the Messiah, giving the world a fresh start by offering forgiveness of sins.... God uses us to persuade men and women to drop their differences and enter into God's work of making things right between them. We're speaking for Christ himself now: Become friends with God; he's already a friend with you' (2 Corinthians 5.19,20 MSG). Can you think of any situations where God has used someone to help others drop their differences and work together?

3. Aristotle said that friendship is based on one of three things:
    a) utility: what each party gets out of it, or
    b) pleasure, through a shared interest, or
    d) the other person's qualities.
        The third of these is the basis for the deepest kind of friendship, which may take a long time to develop, but will be characterised by trust and honesty. Can you trace the progression of Ramanujan's and Hardy's friendship in these categories?

Feedback to the whole group

Closing worship
O God, make speed to save us.
O Lord, make haste to help us.

To you, O Lord, I lift up my soul.
O my God, in you I trust. *(Psalm 25.1)*

1 John 4.7–12
Beloved, let us love one another, because love is from God;
everyone who loves is born of God and knows God. Whoever
does not love does not know God, for God is love. God's love
was revealed among us in this way: God sent his only Son into
the world so that we might live through him. In this is love, not
that we loved God but that he loved us and sent his Son to be
the atoning sacrifice for our sins. Beloved, since God loved us
so much, we also ought to love one another. No one has ever
seen God; if we love one another, God lives in us, and his love
is perfected in us.

Prayers may be offered:
- *for those who work for reconciliation*
- *for those who seek to share God's love*
- *for those in need of a friend*

Thanks be to you, our Lord Jesus Christ,
for all the benefits which you have given us,
for all the pains and insults which you have borne for us.
Most merciful Redeemer, Friend and Brother,
may we know you more clearly,
love you more dearly,
and follow you more nearly,
day by day.
Amen. *(Richard of Chichester, thirteenth century)*

Our Father in heaven,
hallowed be your name,
your kingdom come,
your will be done,
on earth as in heaven.
Give us today our daily bread.
Forgive us our sins
as we forgive those who sin against us.
Lead us not into temptation
but deliver us from evil.
For the kingdom, the power,
and the glory are yours
now and for ever.
Amen.

John 15.12–14
Jesus said, 'This is my commandment, that you love one another as I have loved you. No one has greater love than this, to lay down one's life for one's friends. You are my friends if you do what I command you.'

Go in peace to love and serve the Lord.
In the name of Christ.
Amen.

Questions for personal reflection

1. Where can I locate my friendship with God, over time, within Aristotle's categories?
2. Rabbi Sacks suggests that when Abraham is about to sacrifice Isaac, he is caught in a clear contradiction between God's word to him now and God's word on previous occasions. When two Bible texts appear to contradict each other, how do I resolve the issue?
3. Jesus said: 'I am the vine, you are the branches. He who

abides in Me, and I in him, bears much fruit; for without Me you can do nothing' John 15.5 (NKJV). To abide means to make a home, a permanent base for living. Jesus wants to make his home in our lives, and we can find our home in him. What might need to change in my life to make room for Jesus?

4. Is there someone I need to be reconciled with? Am I prepared for the cost?

Personal Notes...

Week Five: Homeward Bound
Preparatory Reading

God himself will be with them.
Revelation 21.3

In the film, *The Man Who Knew Infinity*, Ramanujan sets out on a hazardous journey to gain a great prize: the publication of his work before he dies. To achieve this, he must face and overcome many obstacles. He finds Cambridge to be very foreign to him, and although it is initially exciting, he finds it frustrating and perplexing, a place of exile. In the end the pull of India is too strong to resist; fearing he may die in England, Ramanujan wants Hardy to promise to get him home. On receiving a distressing letter from Janaki, he works relentlessly to perfect the accuracy of the partitions formula in order to hasten his departure for home.

At the start of this course we thought about our own homes and what they mean to us. We then saw that an experience of exile could be likened to the feeling of not being at home. In this final session we will explore the theme of homecoming by considering where, as Christians, we see our eternal home. One of the most beautiful passages of scripture about homecoming is Jesus' parable of the return of the prodigal son (Luke 15. 11–32). A wayward boy foolishly squanders his inheritance abroad, leaving him destitute and homesick. So he decides to go home, practising a speech that he hopes will turn away his father's wrath and get him a job as a hired hand. When his father, who has been scanning the horizon for any sign of his son, sees him coming, he runs out to greet him throwing his arms around him and kissing him. The son's prepared speech is brushed aside as he is given the best robe to wear, sandals for his feet and a ring for his finger (a sign of belonging). When a party is thrown marking the prodigal's return, the obedient, dutiful elder brother is angry, but the father replies:

'We had to celebrate and rejoice, because this brother of yours was dead and has come to life; he was lost and has been found' (Luke 15.32).

This is perhaps the best loved of all Jesus' parables, showing us a rebellious son welcomed home, with his status restored. Jesus is saying that the father in this parable is just like our heavenly Father, whose love for us is boundless. To be lost is to live as though we are away from that love and gracious forgiveness.

In Week 2 we looked at St Augustine's prayer about the restlessness of the human heart, unsatisfied until it finds its rest in God. He might just as well have said: 'O Lord, we are *homeless* until we find our *home* in You.' Jesus' parable shows us where our heart's true home is to be found. Just like the prodigal we fail to recognise our own beloved status in the eyes of God. Rejecting the one who loves us so completely, we search in far off countries for what is already on our doorstep. However much human love we have known, our deepest need is for our homecoming to God, in our spirits both now and in eternity. Baptism marks the start of the journey of faith to a life lived with God forever. In all likelihood it will include many wanderings from the path, yet the Bible's promise is: 'When you turn to the right or when you turn to the left, your ears shall hear a word behind you, saying, "This is the way; walk in it."' (Isaiah 30.21). And we should remember Jesus' words: 'My sheep hear my voice. I know them, and they follow me' (John 10.27).

There can be many experiences of homecoming with God in this life, but the final homecoming is only reached through the gate of death. When Jesus was preparing his disciples for his death, he reassured them by saying:

'Do not let your hearts be troubled. Believe in God, believe also in me. In my Father's house there are many dwelling-places. If it were not so, would I have told you that I go to prepare a place for you? And if I go and prepare a place for you, I will come again and will take you to myself, so that where I am, there you may be also' (John 14.1–3).

This text has been a source of great comfort and reassurance at countless deathbeds and subsequent funerals.

Everyone, whether a believer or an unbeliever, has a picture of what heaven would be like for them. In his poem *When I'm in heaven* Adrian Plass lists episodes in his life that have felt heavenly; he hopes these will be part of the real thing, such as meeting friends 'in ancient oak-beamed Sussex pubs' (Plass, 1994:101). When I visited York one summer, a local church had set up a blackboard in the street inviting passers-by to write what, for them, heaven on earth should be like. The contributions included: a garden of flowers, food for everyone, a large meal with family and friends, a place of tolerance, a vegan world, and someone had drawn a picture of a rainforest with a sign indicating no entry for humans. Such things speak to us of our hearts' desires and those deepest desires will bring us in touch with the God who truly is the joy of man's desiring. C. S. Lewis draws on this in *The Last Battle* when all the beasts and the children pass through the open doorway into the new Narnia. As they go further in the Unicorn says: 'I have come home at last! This is my country! I belong here. This is the land I have been looking for all my life, though I never knew it till now' (Lewis, 1956:162).

So, what does the Bible have to say about heaven and who is it that will be there? The theologian Paula Gooder has made a close study of the Bible's treatment of heaven and her conclusions will surprise many: she found that there is scant evidence for heaven being the final destination of the dead (see Gooder, 2011). Rather, heaven is God's dwelling place, which he created when he created the earth (Genesis 1.1). Both will eventually cease to be as they are, in their place God will recreate them afresh: 'Then I saw a new heaven and a new earth; for the first heaven and the first earth had passed away, and the sea was no more' (Revelation 21.1). Whatever happens in the interim for the redeemed, their final destination will not be heaven, but a newly created world with God in its midst. That is the dominant picture which the Bible paints:

> And I heard a loud voice from the throne saying,
> 'See, the home of God is among mortals.
> He will dwell with them;
> they will be his peoples,
> and God himself will be with them' (Revelation 21.3).

The concept of resurrection appears quite late in the Hebrew Bible, with the first solid reference to personal resurrection coming as late as the Book of Daniel. In the New Testament, it is St Paul who has most to say on the subject, giving a robust defence of his belief that resurrection will be, as Jesus' was, a bodily resurrection. In the fifteenth chapter of Paul's first letter to the Christians in Corinth, who doubted such a possibility, he speaks of seeds germinating to produce crops of amazing variety, all quite unlike the seeds from which they have grown:

> 'So it is with the resurrection of the dead. What is sown is perishable, what is raised is imperishable. It is sown in dishonour, it is raised in glory. It is sown in weakness, it is raised in power. It is sown a physical body, it is raised a spiritual body. If there is a physical body, there is also a spiritual body' (1 Corinthians 15, 42,44).

Whatever 'a spiritual body' looks like, it is an embodied existence, says Paul, not some ghostly one. Strange though it may sound to some, the New Testament does not paint a picture of a final disembodied existence, but of a resurrection life recognisably embodied, lived out in a new created world where heaven and earth are intertwined. The details of this existence are beyond our imagining, but most importantly we can grasp that it will be a life after death, lived in the presence of God, forever.

Many people struggle with the thought of a bodily resurrection in a newly recreated world. The West has moved away from the biblical understanding of life after death to one influenced more by Greek philosophy: the body being just a temporary lodging for the soul, which at death will leave it behind to experience a disembodied existence. I remember some years ago a BBC interview with the theatre director Jonathan Miller which touched on ideas of life after death. Miller, who thought only oblivion awaited him, spoke eloquently of what he saw as the absurdity of a life without a body. He said that everything he knew about himself had come from being embodied, with all its physical limitations and its 'hereness' rather than its 'thereness'. He was puzzled by the thought of knowing himself after death if he was just some 'thing' without a body. At the time I remember thinking that, if you believe in some kind of resurrection, then this atheist was giving a most powerful argument for it being a bodily resurrection.

Ponder what heaven on earth would mean for you now. What would 'a better country – a heavenly one' have to be like for it to be your heart's true home? What do you understand by the line in The Apostles' Creed: 'I believe in the resurrection of the body'?

The Meeting

Opening worship:
Read again Hebrews 11.13–16 *A better country – a heavenly one*

Recap of last week: Bridging the Gap
The Hardy-Ramanujan partnership had flourished producing outstanding results and their friendship had deepened. Ramanujan's TB had worsened; the letter that finally arrived from Janaki has distressed him, and he longs to go home.

Any further thoughts or questions from last week?

This week: Homeward Bound

Notes about today's first clip:
1. The last days of Ramanujan's visit to England; his return home.
2. Ramanujan has succeeded in producing the mathematical proof that completely validates his partitions formula for every number.
3. Hardy now works to get his friend public recognition. The College had previously refused to give Ramanujan a Fellowship, so now Hardy tries another route: a Fellowship of the Royal Society (FRS), the equivalent of a life-time achievement Oscar, from the oldest, most prestigious, scientific academy (previous Fellows have included such luminaries as Isaac Newton and Charles Darwin).
4. Ramanujan's mother had not posted Janaki's letters to her husband and had intercepted and hidden all of Ramanujan's letters home.

Film Clip 1: 1.27.00–1.32.33 [5.33] *Hardy with the president of the Royal Society – Taxi leaves*

First thoughts: What are your first impressions of this clip?

Whole Group Discussion

1. How might Ramanujan's life have taken a different course if Janaki had joined him in Cambridge?
2. If we sometimes feel we should have taken a different direction in our own lives, is it time wasted, or can it be redeemed? Is it ever too late with God?

Small Group Work

1. Ramanujan was the first Indian to be made a Fellow of the Royal Society and was also its youngest. However, he also knew setbacks, for example, his failure to get a degree in India, and his erroneous formula for primes. For Christians, the disciple Peter is the one we most readily associate with failure. What can failure teach us about ourselves and about God?
2. Ramanujan wanted to end his exile and return to his beloved India. However, it is never possible to go home in the sense of just turning the clock back. People, places and situations, change and move on. Think of a time when you have returned to a hometown, or an old workplace, after a considerable time away. Describe what it was like and how it felt.
3. Has anyone in the group changed their church tradition, or elements of their spirituality, over time? What brought the changes about? What have been the benefits?

Feedback to the whole group

Refreshments

Notes about today's second film clip:

(i) There is now genuine brotherly love between the two men.

(ii) Hardy shows his love by now convincing his colleagues to award a College Fellowship.

(iii) Taxi number 1729 is the smallest number expressible as the sum of two cubes, in two different ways: $1^3 + 12^3$ or $9^3 + 10^3$.

(iv) There is an emotional, painful farewell.

Clip 2: **1.32.34–1.39.08 [6.34]** *Come on the grass... – end credits*

First thoughts: What are your first impressions of this clip?

Whole Group Discussion

1. The Fellowship awards were not enough to hold Ramanujan in Cambridge; his instinct was for the home where his heart was. Share your thoughts of what heaven on earth would be like for you now.

2. Read Revelation 21:1–5. Scripture uses recognisable symbols (a bride and groom, a throne, a Holy City, and so on) to convey an indescribably glorious future. How does this passage speak to you? Share with the group your vision of the future beyond the grave, that 'better country – a heavenly one'.

3. 'If the Gospel omitted all mention of Christ's Resurrection, faith would be easier for me. The Cross by itself suffices me.' So said the French philosopher Simone Weil (1909–43). Why should the resurrection of Jesus Christ be so central to the Christian faith?

4. How do you react to the thought of your own embodied resurrection in a re-created world?

Closing worship
Jesus Christ is the light of the world:
a light no darkness can quench.

Stay with us, Lord, for it is evening:
and the day is almost over.

Jesus Christ came to end our exile:
You give us hope and a home forever.

May the God of hope fill us with joy and peace:
**That we may overflow with hope
by the power of the Holy Spirit.** *(cf John 1.5; Luke 24.29; Romans 15.13)*

John 20.24–29
A week later his disciples were again in the house, and Thomas was with them. Although the doors were shut, Jesus came and stood among them and said, 'Peace be with you.' Then he said to Thomas, 'Put your finger here and see my hands. Reach out your hand and put it in my side. Do not doubt but believe.' Thomas answered him, 'My Lord and my God!' Jesus said to him, 'Have you believed because you have seen me? Blessed are those who have not seen and yet have come to believe.'

Prayers may be offered:
- *for those downcast by disappointments or failures*
- *for grace to grasp the wonder of Christ with us, now and always*
- *for a deeper appreciation of the future hope we have in Christ*

O gracious and holy Father,
give us wisdom to perceive you,
diligence to seek you,
patience to wait for you,
eyes to behold you,
a heart to meditate upon you,
and a life to proclaim you,
through the power of the Spirit

of Jesus Christ our Lord. *(Benedict of Nursia, c.550)*

The grace of our Lord Jesus Christ,
and the love of God,
and the fellowship of the Holy Spirit,
be with us all evermore. Amen.

Go in the hope and the power of the resurrection.
Amen.

Questions for personal reflection

1. Where do I look for unconditional love?
2. Read Luke 15.11–32. In what ways am I like the prodigal son? As I imagine myself into the scene, what do I want to say to the Father? How does he receive me?
3. Is death only something to be dreaded, or can I rejoice in it being the gateway to my heart's true home?
4. At the end of this five-week course, what have I learned about myself and about God? What do I want to give thanks for today?

Personal Notes...

Postscript

These final pages contain further thoughts for reflection on big questions that *The Man Who Knew Infinity* might raise. It can be used as resource material for a post-course meeting, say after Easter. There are some discussion starters provided; some groups may wish to focus on particular sections. There are two sections included for those who are keen for some mathematics!

Christians and Hindus

Ramanujan and Hardy were polar opposites; they each came from a culture that was totally alien to the other. One was a dry, intellectual Englishman, cut off from his emotions and convinced that there is no God, the other a passionate young Indian, who 'danced with numbers to infinity' and believed in a personal Hindu goddess who spoke to him in dreams. Neither had seen anything quite like the other before, their only common ground seemed to be their consuming love for mathematics. And yet each was able to see the humanity in the other, providing the ground for a deep friendship to develop.

Hinduism is a term coined by the British to cover the complexity of beliefs and practices that they encountered during their time as rulers of India. It is not a single, organised religion, but a great variety of beliefs and different traditions; there is not just one way of being a Hindu. Brahman, the ultimate reality, the divine consciousness, is the final ground of all that is. Within Hinduism there are many gods and goddesses, most notably the Triumvirate of Brahma, the creator of the universe, Vishnu, the preserver and protector of it, and Shiva, its destroyer. Namagiri, the goddess Ramanujan said spoke to him, is a form of Lakshmi, the goddess of good fortune. Do Hindus therefore worship many gods or one God? The picture is somewhat confusing: some Hindus say that there is only one God (Brahman), the others are only manifestations or embodiments of this one God. Other Hindus, whilst respecting other gods, are devoted to a particular family or village god/goddess, who takes a supreme position. Still other Hindus believe that there are truly many gods who can be approached at different times. All living creatures have souls which are each part of the supreme soul. The goal of Hinduism is to achieve *moksha*, freedom from the endless cycle of death and rebirth (reincarnation), to become part of the absolute soul, one with Brahman. This is achieved through the path one follows through life to reduce, and one day, finally eliminate bad *karma*, the wrong actions that inevitably lead to rebirth.

On the face of it, Hinduism and Christianity have absolutely nothing in common. The apparent worship of images, idols, and multiple deities repels most Christians, whereas Christianity's focus on the one historical figure Jesus Christ, and its exclusive claims, makes Christianity appear an inferior religion to Hindus, whose own faith claims total inclusivity with everything else. Can there be any dialogue between these two religions?

Father Bede Griffiths (1906–1993) was an English Benedictine monk who lived much of his life in Southern India and was a major figure in the Christian Ashram Movement. His life's work was to discover his deepest Christian identity through exposure to the Hindu religion and culture, and to encourage conversations between the two. Never compromising his faith in Christ, Griffiths attracted many by his teaching, both those from the west, disillusioned with much of the organised Church, and those within India itself, who saw in Griffiths a western prophet bringing fresh insights to their lives.

Griffiths insisted that not all religions are the same, but, although they can be deeply conflicted on the surface, by discovering their depths one could see a unity behind them. Like the fingers of a hand, each world religion is unique and distinctive, but they all converge on the palm, on the centre.

Each is a stepping stone to a deeper reality, which lies beyond them all.

Griffiths said that Hinduism had given him a profound sense of the sacredness of all life. He saw that it has much to teach about the inner life of the spirit, and a depth of awareness of God that very few Christians in the west have today. He believed Christians can learn from India the value of a simpler lifestyle, that is less distracted and which can lead to greater wholeness and peace. However, he also saw that Christians have something of great importance to bring to their Hindu neighbours: a spirituality based on love.

Hinduism is based on the transformation of consciousness, and its followers aim to reach that state in which you become one with the supreme being, the supreme reality, where there is pure consciousness, absolute bliss, and transcendence. The danger, said Griffiths, is that the Hindu's concern for their own union with the supreme being lacks any expression of love, and there is no sense of relationship about it. Concern for the suffering of others may then be reduced. The gift that Christian spirituality can bring is its insistence on the centrality of love, a communion of love with God, a love which comes from God and is to be shared with the whole of creation.

Bede Griffiths lamented the fact that the universal tolerance that Hinduism had always exemplified in the past was now giving way to an aggressive, politicised Hindu fundamentalism, which identified Indian identity very much with being a Hindu. This has caused much tension between the majority Hindus, and the far smaller populations of Muslims and Christians. This conflict is compounded for Indian Christians as they can be linked with the colonialism of the past.

In the west Hindus and Christians can meet on more level terms, as equals. The Christian is called to see each person they meet as a child of God, made in his image, a neighbour to love as ourselves. The Hindu greets the stranger with the Namaste gesture, meaning 'I bow to the divine in you' or 'the sacred in me bows to the sacred in you'. Recognising and encountering each other as created with a divine spark, is perhaps the most fruitful ground on which Christians and Hindus can start a conversation – fellow human beings, fellow citizens, and, possibly spiritual friends.

God the mathematician

Forty minutes into the film Hardy questions Ramanujan about his motives for pursuing mathematics. The young man says that he is compelled to do it because he sees the beauty of it. There is no suggestion that his interest lies in its utility, as an engineer might view her mathematics, but Ramanujan has the passion and vision of an artist, captivated by its form, structure and beauty. In his book *A Mathematician's Apology* Hardy very much agrees: his interest, too, lay in its aesthetic appeal rather than its utility.

However, as the film ends, we are told of the discovery of a lost Ramanujan notebook 'containing ground-breaking formulas' which are helping scientists today to understand the behaviour of black holes. It does seem most extraordinary, and worth pondering, that the pursuit of mathematics for art's sake alone, should one day find application in an area of science no one had even dreamed of at the time. In fact, this is by no means a rare occurrence: mathematical structures seem to be deeply built into the fabric of the world. The physicist Eugene Wigner coined the phrase 'the unreasonable effectiveness of mathematics', and the physicist and theologian John Polkinghorne has spoken of its power to unlock the secrets of the physical universe. It is no wonder that another physicist, Freeman Dyson, should have quipped that: 'there seems to be a rule, that anything mathematicians can invent, God can somehow use' (Dyson, 1998). It is surely quite remarkable that the mathematics humans have developed to model the motions of such observable things as cannonballs, rockets, and planets, should also become a powerful tool for revealing the unseen realms of atoms and quarks or what happened during the first moments of creation. Whilst this does not constitute a knock down argument for the existence of God, it is at least an interesting observation worthy of serious notice.

As we have seen Hardy and Littlewood were aghast at the Indian's lack of concern for proofs of his results. The film leaves us wondering where Ramanujan's discoveries came from. Were they the products of his own highly intuitive imagination, or were they divine revelations? Freeman Dyson's own conclusion was that Ramanujan must have had access to some 'magic tricks' that we just don't understand.

The gap between truth and proof

Ramanujan and Hardy clashed over the need for proof in their work in mathematics. A decade after Ramanujan returned to India a young Austrian logician, Kurt Gödel (1906–1978), made the biggest mathematical discovery of the twentieth century, showing that there is a paradox at the heart of mathematics. Put simply, there are probably mathematical truths which mathematics can ever prove. This is not because we are not clever enough, but because there is an incompleteness inherent in mathematics which effectively limits its power. This unwelcome fact rocked the world of mathematics and, subsequently, has had serious implications for all the mathematical sciences.

All mathematics is constructed on the foundations of a set of axioms, simple building blocks on which the superstructure is erected. These axioms are the things we *believe* to be true about the ways that numbers work. For example, in arithmetic, one of the axioms is that it doesn't matter what order you add up a list of numbers, you'll always get the same result ($5 + 8 + 2 = 8 + 2 + 5$ and so on). Using the full set of axioms, mathematicians use logic to reason and deduce everything else that constitutes the subject. The important point to notice is that the axioms are *presumed* to be true and sufficient in number to allow mathematics to proceed in a useful and reliable way. The axioms must be what is called 'consistent', that is they shouldn't lead to contradictory results. That we have such a system has been believed since the time of the ancient Greeks, and that it supports a mathematics which is capable enough to deduce everything that there is to know about the subject. But in 1931 Gödel produced his 'incompleteness theorem', which showed mathematics has an Achilles' heel: he showed that not all truths in mathematics may be accessible by the system.

You might ask that if the current axioms aren't sufficient for the job, why not add another new axiom to the set, one we are pretty sure is true? No, said Gödel, that won't solve the basic problem, adding new axioms just creates new systems, which will be subject to their own limitations of incompleteness, possibly leaving some matters unprovable. And anyway, what might these additional axioms be, that we are prepared to trust them?

The inescapable conclusion is that there is a boundary to what mathematicians know, beyond which may lie mathematical truths that are not susceptible to proof. As mathematician Marcus du Sautoy has remarked there is a 'gap between truth and proof', even in the field of numbers! This was a great shock for all mathematicians because they had looked upon their subject as being immune to uncertainties.

A possible example of this uncertainty might be the so called Goldbach Conjecture. In 1742 the German mathematician Christian Goldbach stated that every even number greater than 2 can be written as the sum of two primes:

4 = 2 + 2 2 is a prime
6 = 3 + 3 3 is a prime
8 = 3 + 5 3 and 5 are both primes

10 = 3 + 7 3 and 7 are both primes
12 = 5 + 7 5 and 7 are both primes
Etc.

It looks so simple and intuitively true! But is it true beyond all doubt for *every* even number, however big? Goldbach didn't leave us a proof.

We could spend the rest of our lives testing examples to see if we can find an exception that proves Goldbach wrong, but to date, no one has, not even with the biggest computers. However, that doesn't make it true beyond all doubt. Mathematicians like G. H. Hardy would not have been satisfied. He would say that intuition can only take us so far, what is needed is rigorous proof.

Mathematicians have laboured long and hard to show that Goldbach's conjecture is either true or false, but without success. Some are now beginning to wonder if it is not a case of the dreaded Gödelian Achilles' heel: Goldbach's Conjecture is true, but there is no route to a solution, we will never be able to prove it.

The limitations of science

There is a great deal of work going on in the fields of theoretical physics, astronomy, and cosmology that is totally dependent upon mathematics. There is a well-publicised quest for a Theory of Everything which achieves the unification of Einstein's General Relativity (the physics of stars, galaxies, and black holes) and Quantum Mechanics (the physics of small subatomic particles of matter, like quarks and gluons). The best attempt right now seems to be the so-called String Theory. If such a theory should be found, will the scientists be able to sit back and say: 'job well done, now we know it all'? In his book *A Brief History of Time*, Stephen Hawking imagined that a human triumph as great as a complete theory would be akin to knowing the mind of God.

However, the scientist, theologian and Benedictine priest Stanley Jaki has bemoaned such physicists' strange reluctance to recognise the implications of Gödel's theorem for any final formulation of a theory of everything. Physicists can never say that their beautiful theories will not be overturned by future experimental observations. Neither is a theory with apparent mathematical perfection protected from the possibility that it fails to be a complete picture of reality. Precisely because of Gödel's theorem there will be no end to physics (see Jaki, 2006: 55).

Much modern cosmology is based on mathematical extrapolations – going wherever the equations take us. This has resulted in speculation about such things as multiverses, the loss of free will, and the illusion of time. These are little more than metaphysical speculations, for they fail to meet Karl Popper's criterion for the falsifiable nature of true science: any theory must be capable of being disproved by observation and experiment. And Gödel's theorem means that our mathematical systems *may* be incomplete, which should at least keep us humble and aware of claiming to know too much.

If physicists do ever achieve their goal of finding a theory that can unify all the forces of the universe, it will be a truly magnificent achievement, but it won't be the final word and it certainly won't be the death of God. What it will be is further evidence of coherence and intelligibility at the heart of the universe, a compelling sign of a rational creator. And it will further support Galileo's conviction that the laws of nature are written by the hand of God in the language of mathematics.

Science and Religion

Some things will always lie beyond us and we should have the humility to recognise that:

'For my thoughts are not your thoughts, nor are your ways my ways, says the Lord. For as the heavens are higher than the earth, so are my ways higher than your ways and my thoughts than your thoughts' (Isaiah 55.8,9).

The scientific method has been phenomenally successful in discovering *how* the world works, but it cannot answer 'the riddles of existence', questions of meaning and purpose. Such questions remain the province of religion and revelation. If physicists, chemists and food nutritionists study a recently baked cake they can tell us its physical make-up, the changes undergone in the baking process, its nutritional value, etc., but they cannot tell us who it was for, or for what occasion it was made. For a complete explanation, the cook must be sought to reveal the answer. Scientists tell us all about how the world works, but their descriptions lack an important ingredient: the purpose behind it all.

We need the wisdom to recognise that there are other important ways of knowing that are beyond the reach of the sciences. Even the most materialist scientist doesn't prove her husband's love for her by examining it under a microscope; nor does she appreciate the beauty of a Mozart symphony by analysing the peaks and troughs of recorded soundwaves; she relies on other ways of knowing. Our knowledge of beauty and love, human or divine, is not accessed through science.

Equally, the knowledge of what is good and evil, right and wrong, and what constitutes wise action, are all important ways of knowing that are necessary for our wellbeing, that do not come from science. To live well and to have a fuller, more satisfying account of human existence, we need to recognise that science does not hold all the answers.

Some advances in science have clearly challenged traditional religious beliefs, but conflict cannot be used as the overriding description of the relationship between science and religion. The advances don't herald the end of religious belief, rather they can be windows onto a deeper reality. The physicist and priest John Polkinghorne writes: 'Science without religion is incomplete; it fails to attain the deepest possible understanding.... The dialogue between them can only be mutually enriching' (Polkinghorne, 1988: 97).

Science and faith are not rivals for the truth, but partners, each dealing with a different aspect of the same truth: one at the level of mechanism, the other at the level of meaning. Questions like 'how did everything begin?', 'what are we here for, and what is the point of life?', are amongst the most interesting that can be asked. These must be addressed not only on a scientific level, but also on the level of meaning and purpose.

Group Discussion Questions

Christians and Hindus

1. Do you have personal contact with any Hindus? Have you ever visited a Hindu Temple? What have you learned of their faith? What more would you like to know about their lifestyle, practices, or concept of an afterlife?

2. Bede Griffiths said that everything we can say about God is limited, symbolic, an analogy pointing towards an inexpressible mystery. To what extent do you agree with him? What grounds for a dialogue between Christians and Hindus do you see?

3. Hinduism's multiplicity of gods and goddesses could be likened to the spokes of a wheel, each emanating from the hub, playing their own individual roles. How would you defend Christianity from the accusation that its own trinitarian faith amounts to belief in three gods?

Mathematics

4. Mathematics has a very dry image, off-putting to many,

so what makes this film so compelling?

5. Mathematics might be said to be a human construct which helps us make sense of our everyday world. But do you see any significance in the fact that scientists are discovering 'the unreasonable effectiveness of mathematics', even down to the subatomic level, of which we have no direct experience?

6. Are you able to conceive that Ramanujan's 'magic tricks' were the result of divine revelations?

Science and Religion

7. A mathematician looks for a rigorous proof, i.e., a watertight argument, based on agreed rules of logic, using the accepted axioms. How do we prove the truth of important things in our own lives, like friendship, love, honesty and faithfulness?

8. Richard Dawkins says that God is a delusion: faith is blind trust in the absence of any evidence, an infantile deception akin to the Tooth Fairy. How would you answer him?

9. Francis Collins, one time leader of the Human Genome Project, has said that his science and his Christian faith come together to form 'an intellectually and spiritually satisfying synthesis' of great truths. Do the big discoveries in science threaten to weaken or enhance your faith?

And finally...

10. Looking back over the course, what have been the highlights?

About the Author

Andy Colebrooke is a retired Anglican priest with thirty years ministerial experience, serving two incumbencies in Chelmsford Diocese and being Rural Dean of Harwich. He is an experienced leader and deviser of Lent and other short courses and has been a tutor on Chelmsford's Course in Christian Studies. He attended Imperial College, London to study Physics before doing postgraduate research in Polymer Physics (Ph.D. 1975). Prior to ordination he taught Reactor Physics at Queen Mary College, London, followed by more than a decade teaching mathematics in secondary schools. With a conviction that science and faith need not be enemies, but rather together provide a rich harmony of understanding, he is the author of *Science and Religion*, which explores the spirituality of the Victorian physicist James Clerk Maxwell, sometimes dubbed 'The Scottish Einstein'. Andy now lives in Saffron Walden in Essex with his wife, Hazel and they delight in having three grown-up children and seven amazing grandchildren.

References

Bollobás B. (2020) Srinivasa Ramanujan, *The Personal Friend of Every Integer*, Cambridge: Trinity College Annual Record 2019–2020.

Coffey J. (1999) Engaging with cinema, *Cambridge Papers*, vol. 8, no. 1, [Online]. Available at https://www.jubilee-centre.org/cambridge-papers/engaging-with-cinema (Accessed 10 July 2021).

Craik D. M. *A Life for a Life* (1859) [Online] Available at https://archive.org/details/lifeforlife00crairich/page/n5/mode/1up?view=theater (Accessed 15 July 2021).

Dickens C. (1854) Hard Times, London: Bradbury & Evans (this edition 1995 London: Penguin Classics).

Dyson F. (1998) *God appears to be a Mathematician* [Online]. Available at www.webofstories.com/play/freeman.dyson/148 (Accessed 21 June 2021).

Grahame K. (1908) *The Wind in the Willows*, London: Methuen (this edition 2016 London: Egmont Books).

Gooder P. (2011) *Heaven*, London: SPCK.

Hardy G.H. (1920) 'Obituary: S. Ramanujan F.R.S.', *Nature*, vol. 105, no. 2642, pp. 494–495.

Jaki S. L. (2006) *On a Discovery about Gödel's Incompleteness Theorem* [Online]. Available at www.pas.va/content/dam/accademia/pdf/acta18/acta18-jaki.pdf (Accessed 24 June 2021).

Kanigel R. (2016) *The Man Who Knew Infinity*, London: Abacas

Kipling R. (1890) 'Gunga Din', *New York Tribune* 22 May. Available in *Rudyard Kipling - Selected Poems*, London: Penguin Classics (2000).

Lewis C. S. (1956) *The Last Battle*, London: The Bodley Head Ltd, (this edition 1980 London: Fontana Lions).

Mitchell G. J. (1999) *Making Peace*, London: Random House.

Mursell G. (2005) *Praying in Exile*, London: Darton, Longman and Todd.

Packer J. I. (1973) *Knowing God*, London: Hodder and Stoughton Ltd.

Plass A. (1994) The Unlocking, Oxford: The Bible Reading Fellowship.

Polkinghorne J. (1988) *Science and Creation*, London: SPCK.

Sacks J. (2019) 'Negative Capability', *The Office of Rabbi Sacks*, 11 November 2019 [Blog]. Available at https://rabbisacks.org/vayera-5780/ (Accessed 21 June 2021).

Smail T. (1995) *Windows on the Cross*, London: Darton, Longman and Todd.

Trinity College Chapel (2021) *Memorial Brasses in the Ante-Chapel* [Online]. Available at www.trinitycollegechapel.com/about/memorials/brasses/ (Accessed on 23 June 2021).

For Further Reading
The Man Who Knew Infinity by Robert Kanigel, Abacas 1991. The book on which the film is based.

A Mathematician's Apology by G.H. Hardy, Cambridge University Press, 1940 (latest printing 2012).

The Meeting of Opposites? Hindus and Christians in the West by Andrew Wingate, SPCK 2014.

For more about Father Bede Griffiths see: *A Human Search: The Life of Father Bede Griffiths* (1993) Directed by John Swindells, More than Illusion Films (Australia).

The Language of God: a scientist presents evidence for belief by Francis Collins, Pocket Books 2007.

The Film
The Man Who Knew Infinity (2015) Directed by Matt Brown. Warner Bros. Pictures (United Kingdom) Mister Smith Entertainment (International).

CIRCLE
BOOKS

CHRISTIAN FAITH

Circle Books explores a wide range of disciplines within the field of Christian faith and practice. It also draws on personal testimony and new ways of finding and expressing God's presence in the world today.

If you have enjoyed this book, why not tell other readers by posting a review on your preferred book site. Recent bestsellers from Circle Books are:

I Am With You (Paperback)
John Woolley

These words of divine encouragement were given to John Woolley in his work as a hospital chaplain, and have since inspired and uplifted tens of thousands, even changed their lives.
Paperback: 978-1-90381-699-8 ebook: 978-1-78099-485-7

God Calling
A. J. Russell

365 messages of encouragement channelled from Christ to two anonymous "Listeners".
Hardcover: 978-1-905047-42-0 ebook: 978-1-78099-486-4

The Long Road to Heaven,
A Lent Course Based on the Film
Tim Heaton
This second Lent resource from the author of *The Naturalist and the Christ* explores Christian understandings of "salvation" in a five-part study based on the film *The Way*.
Paperback: 978-1-78279-274-1 ebook: 978-1-78279-273-4

Abide In My Love
More Divine Help for Today's Needs
John Woolley
The companion to *I Am With You*, *Abide In My Love* offers words of divine encouragement.
Paperback: 978-1-84694-276-1

From the Bottom of the Pond
The Forgotten Art of Experiencing God in the Depths of the Present Moment
Simon Small
From the Bottom of the Pond takes us into the depths of the present moment, to the only place where God can be found.
Paperback: 978-1-84694-066-8 ebook: 978-1-78099-207-5

God Is A Symbol Of Something True
Why You Don't Have to Choose Either a Literal Creator God or a Blind, Indifferent Universe
Jack Call
In this examination of modern spiritual dilemmas, Call offers the explanation that some of the most important elements of life are beyond our control: everything is fundamentally alright.
Paperback: 978-1-84694-244-0

The Scarlet Cord
Conversations With God's Chosen Women
Lindsay Hardin Freeman, Karen N. Canton
Voiceless wax figures no longer, twelve biblical women,
outspoken, independent, faithful, selfless risk-takers, come to life
in *The Scarlet Cord*.
Paperback: 978-1-84694-375-1

Will You Join in Our Crusade?
The Invitation of the Gospels Unlocked by the Inspiration of
Les Miserables
Steve Mann
Les Miserables' narrative is entwined with Bible study in this book
of 42 daily readings from the Gospels, perfect for Lent or anytime.
Paperback: 978-1-78279-384-7 ebook: 978-1-78279-383-0

A Quiet Mind
Uniting Body, Mind and Emotions in Christian Spirituality
Eva McIntyre
A practical guide to finding peace in the present moment that will
change your life, heal your wounds and bring you a quiet mind.
Paperback: 978-1-84694-507-6 ebook: 978-1-78099-005-7

Readers of ebooks can buy or view any of these bestsellers by
clicking on the live link in the title. Most titles are published in
paperback and as an ebook. Paperbacks are available in traditional
bookshops. Both print and ebook formats are available online.

Find more titles and sign up to our readers' newsletter at http://
www.johnhuntpublishing.com/christianity. Follow us on Facebook
at https://www.facebook.com/ChristianAlternative.